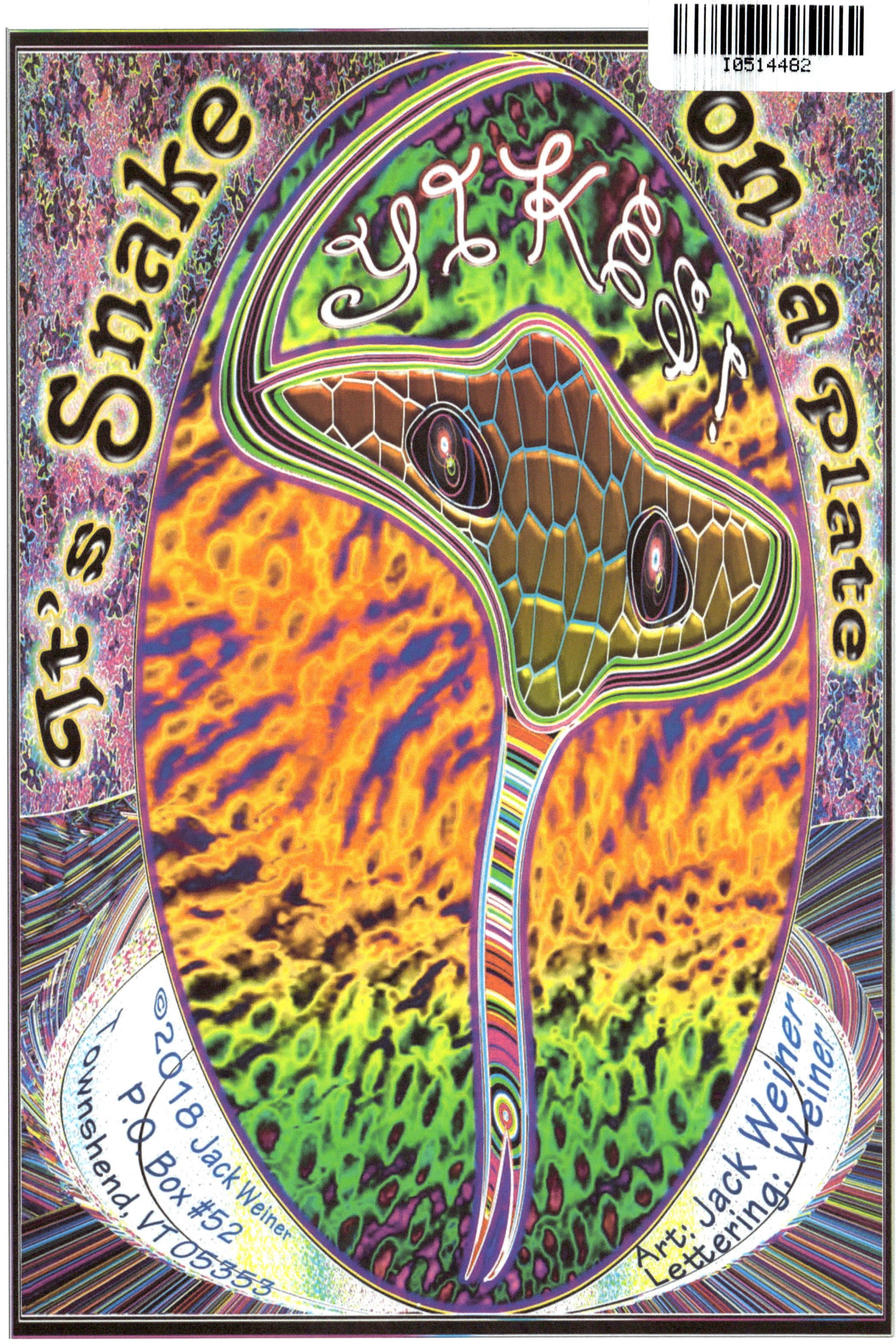

Some things to consider

1. **ALWAYS** treat **all** snakes with respect and gratitude for the role they play in the Natural World. Especially, when one is hissing at you!

2. **ALWAYS** research which snakes, in your locality, may be on the **Endangered Species List** BEFORE you are in a situation which could require killing one: berry picking, hiking, camping, fishing, rock-climbing, **yard-work,** etc. Sometimes, snakes will appear in the most unlikely places, from the outdoor swimming pool, to the kitchen floor or broom closet; so, learn to identify the types of snakes in your local area and State. Some Endangered Species are dangerous.

3. **NEVER** pick up any live snake unless you are **100% POSITIVE** that it is NON-VENOMOUS; or, you have special training and experience in identifying and safely handling venomous snakes. **DO NOT KILL** or injure a snake if you can help it. Should you ever need to dispatch a live snake, BE HUMANE about it and don't cause the animal unnecessary suffering.

4. **REMEMBER**, many types of snakes are beneficial; especially on farms, where they consume many rodents and insects. Non-poisonous King Snakes will kill and consume poisonous species of snakes that try to invade their territory, as well as many types of destructive rodents. Learn to identify the King Snakes in your locale.

5. **NEVER** eat a "Road Kill" snake", since it will harbor some very nasty bacteria.

6. **IT IS RECOMMENDED** that the head of a venomous snake be removed before cooking, since the head is where the poison producing glands are located.

7. **ALWAYS** prepare and consume the fresh snake meat as soon as possible; or, the meat can be packaged and frozen, dried and smoked, or made into Jerky for later use. **CLEANLINESS is the RULE**.

8. **IF YOU DON'T** want to hunt down and kill a snake, there is an easy alternative...the Internet. There are several very reputable venders that produce and sell a variety of snake meats especially selected for cooking and consuming. **GOOGLE** "Mail Order Snake Meat". You'll discover a whole new world of exotic foods. Of course, always do rigorous research *before* buying.

THE DANGERS OF CONSUMING SNAKE MEAT INCLUDE;

1. **Risk of Being Killed by Residual Venom**

    There's always the danger of consuming snake venom especially from **UNDER-COOKED or RAW** snake meat. Eating inappropriately prepared snake meats can result in serious medical complications.

2. **Danger of Pricks from Poisonous or Venom Contaminated Bones**

    The network of snake bones is very extensive and preparing a snakes meat, for cooking, is an acquired Art which most people have not mastered. The bones of many snake species could still be poisonous from contamination even after death. This makes handling of snake meat by an inexperienced cook very dangerous.

3. **Danger of Bite Even After Death**

    The reflexive action of the nervous system of many snake species allows them to bite and inject venom even after death. This feat is common in snakes like Cobras and Rattlesnakes.

4. **Microbiological and Heavy Metal Contamination**

    Eating reptiles can pose serious health challenges as a result of the presence of parasites, bacteria, viruses and **heavy metals**; like **Mercury**. A study published in the **International Journal of Food Microbiology** revealed that eating reptiles such as snakes can result in **Trichinosis, Pentastomiasis, Gnathostomiasis and Sparganosis. According to Simone Magnino,** the lead author of the study and a researcher for the **World Health Organization (WHO),** the greatest risk comes from the presence of **Salmonella, Shgella, Escherichia coli, Yersinia enterolitica, Campylobacter, Clostridium and Staphylococcus aureus,** which can result in severe illnesses and disease.

    Snake Meat may "taste like chicken" but it is **NOT** chicken, it may appear cheap but in the long run the cost of medical care and its hassles can often be an unjustifiable burden. Sometimes, when it comes to snakes, the wisest course of action is to safely incinerate, bury, or properly dispose its carcass; after it's dead, of course. **Be SAFE not SORRY.**

    If you are determined to hunt a snake for possible consumption, my advice is this; <u>thoroughly</u> educate yourself about snakes, especially the species which you may encounter on your hunt. **STAY ALERT...STAY ALIVE.**

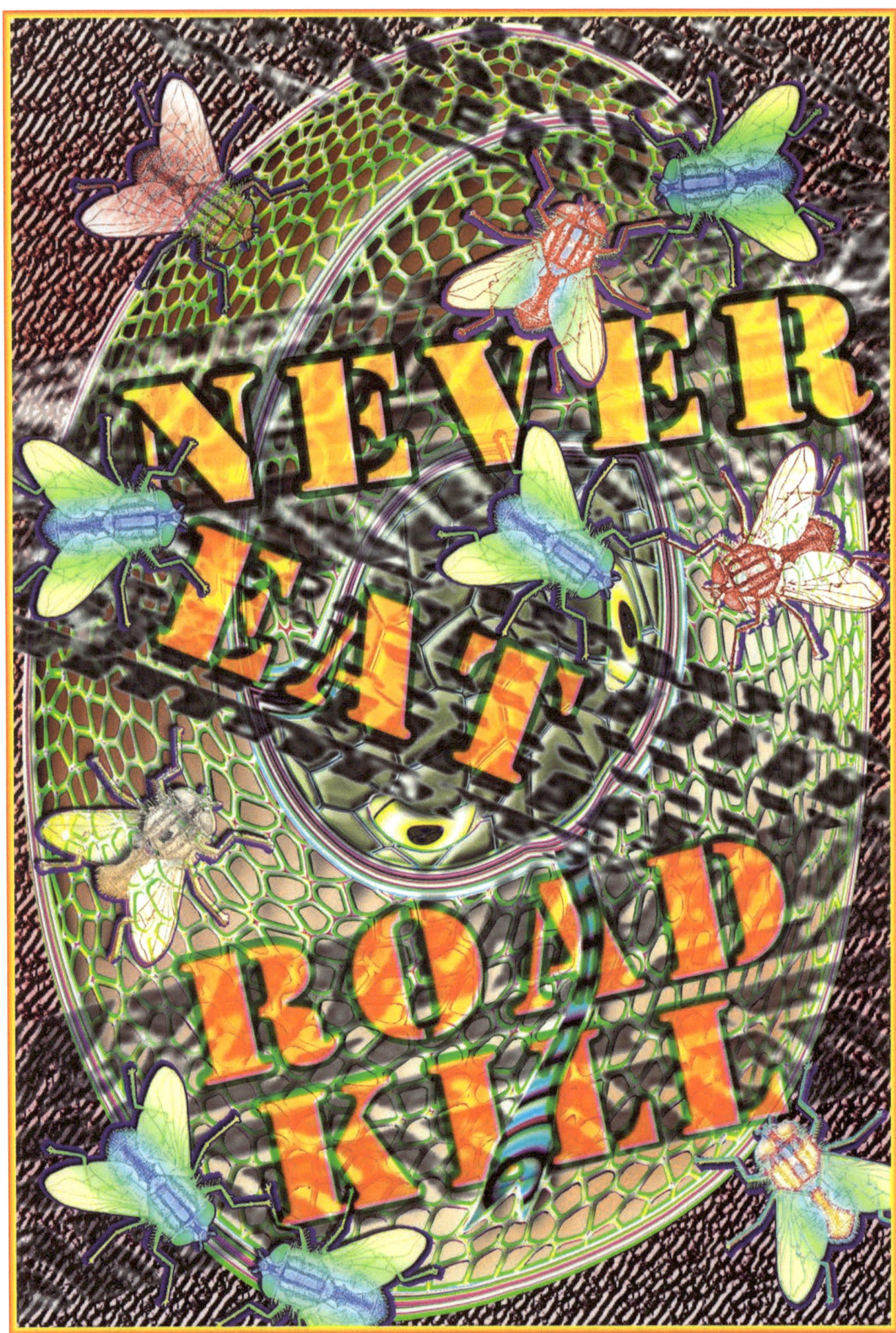

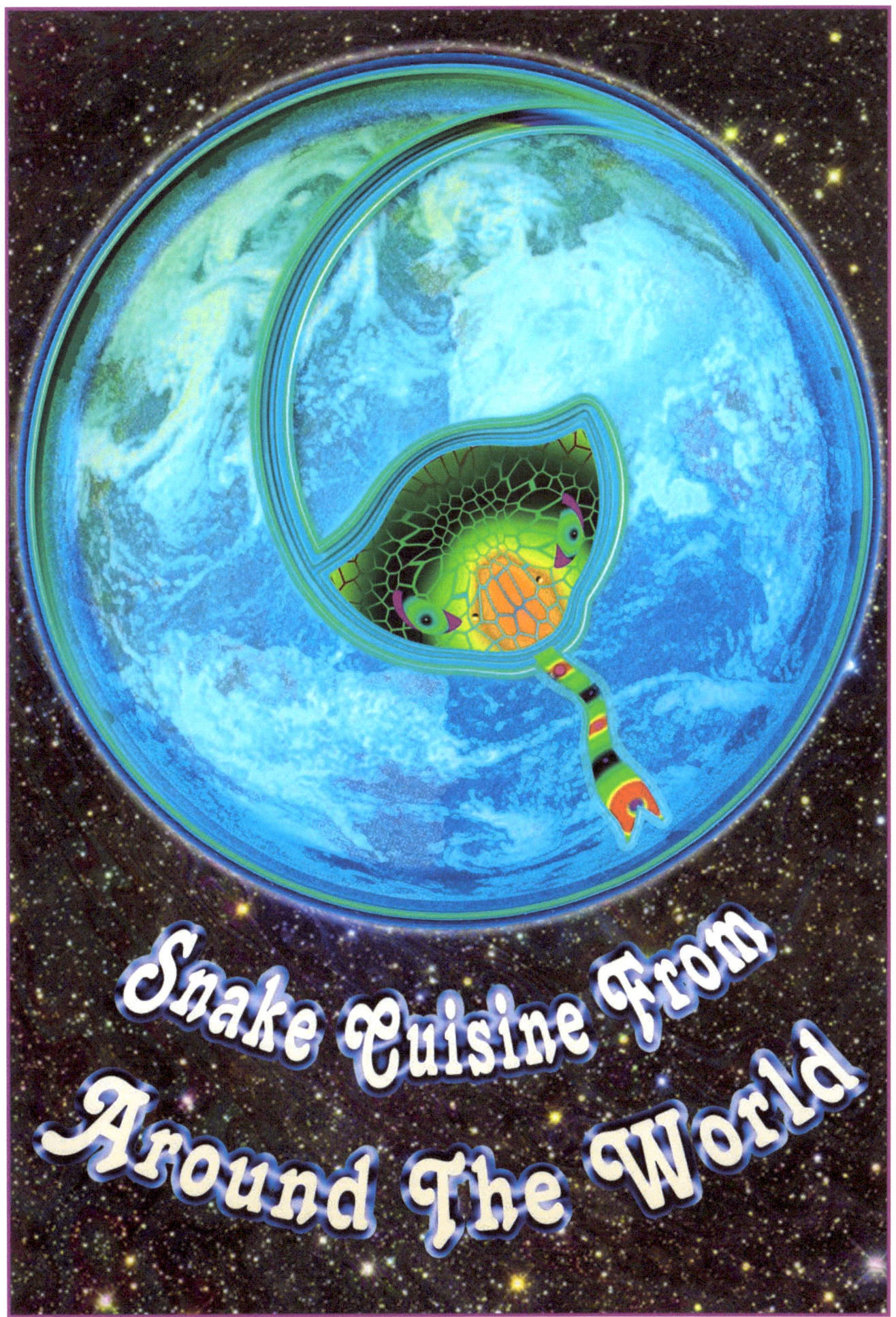

Snake Basics

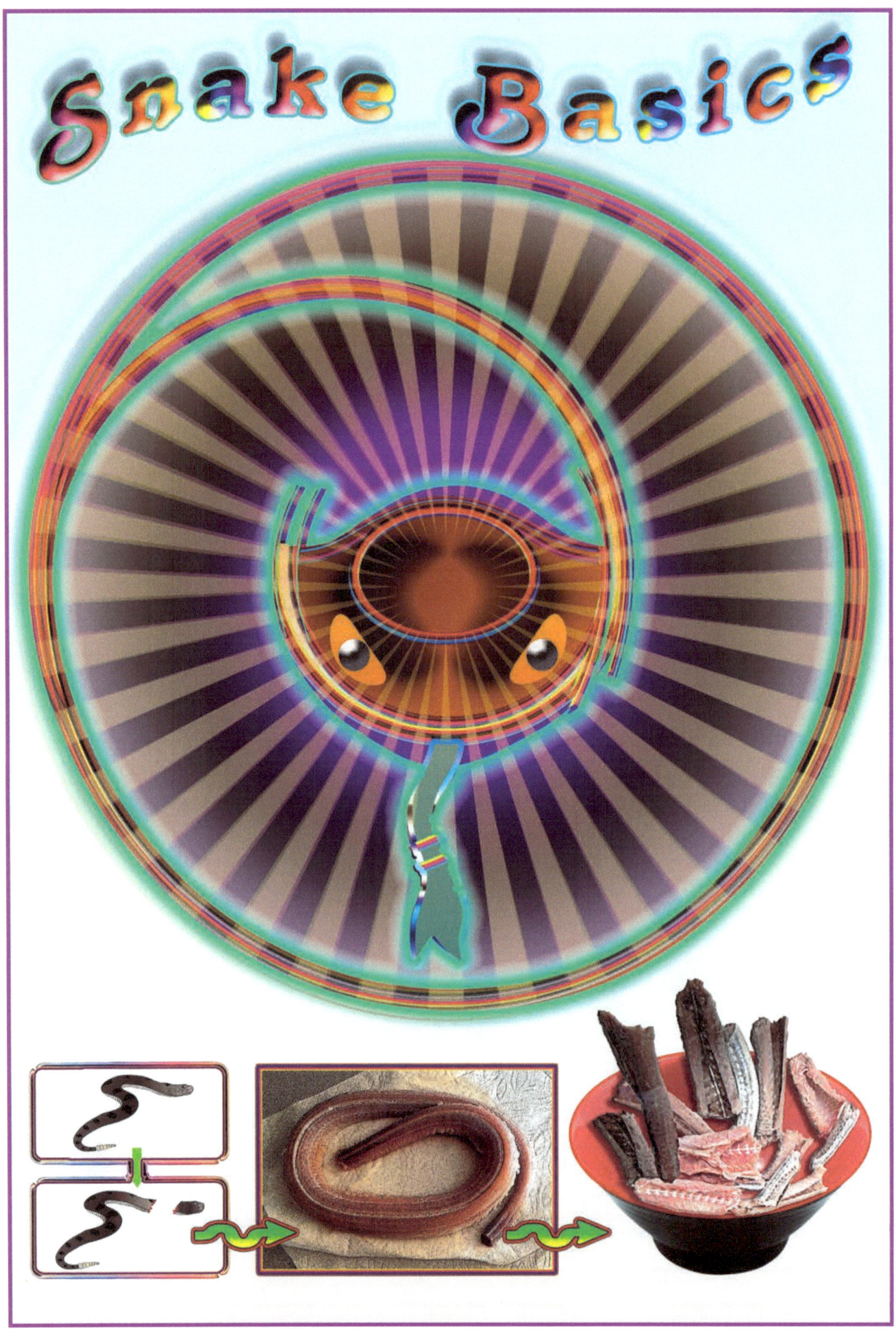

6

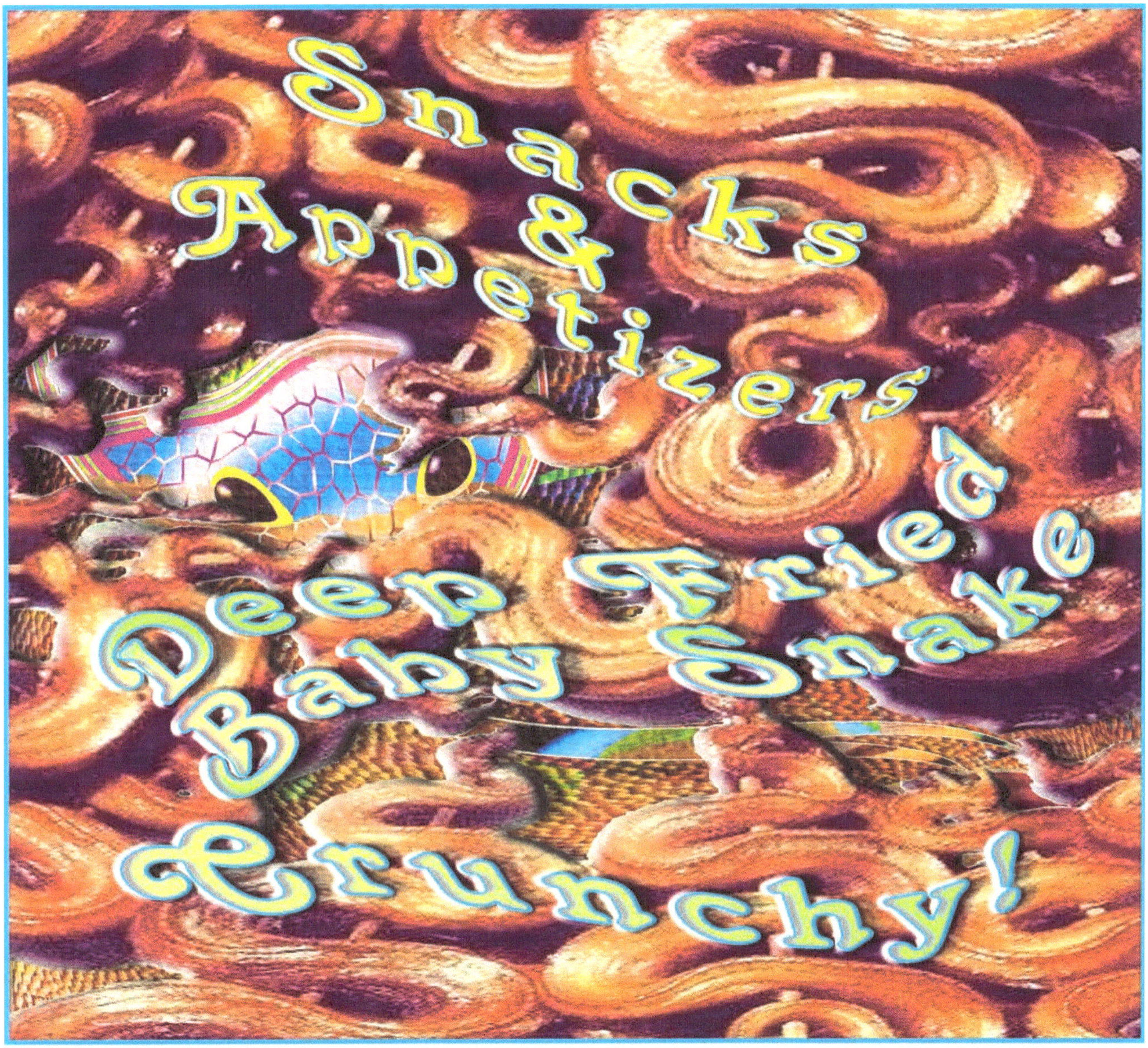

Snacks & Appetizers

Deep Fried Baby Snake
Crunchy!

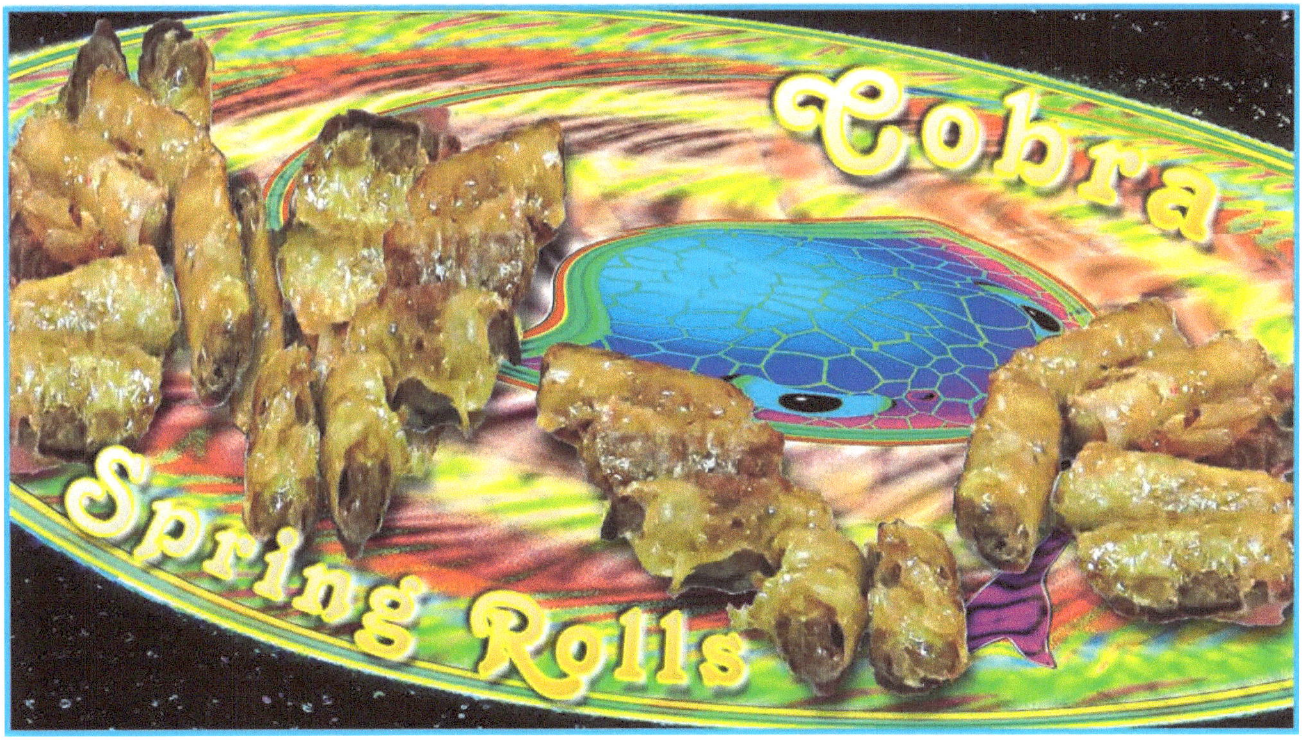

Cobra Spring Rolls

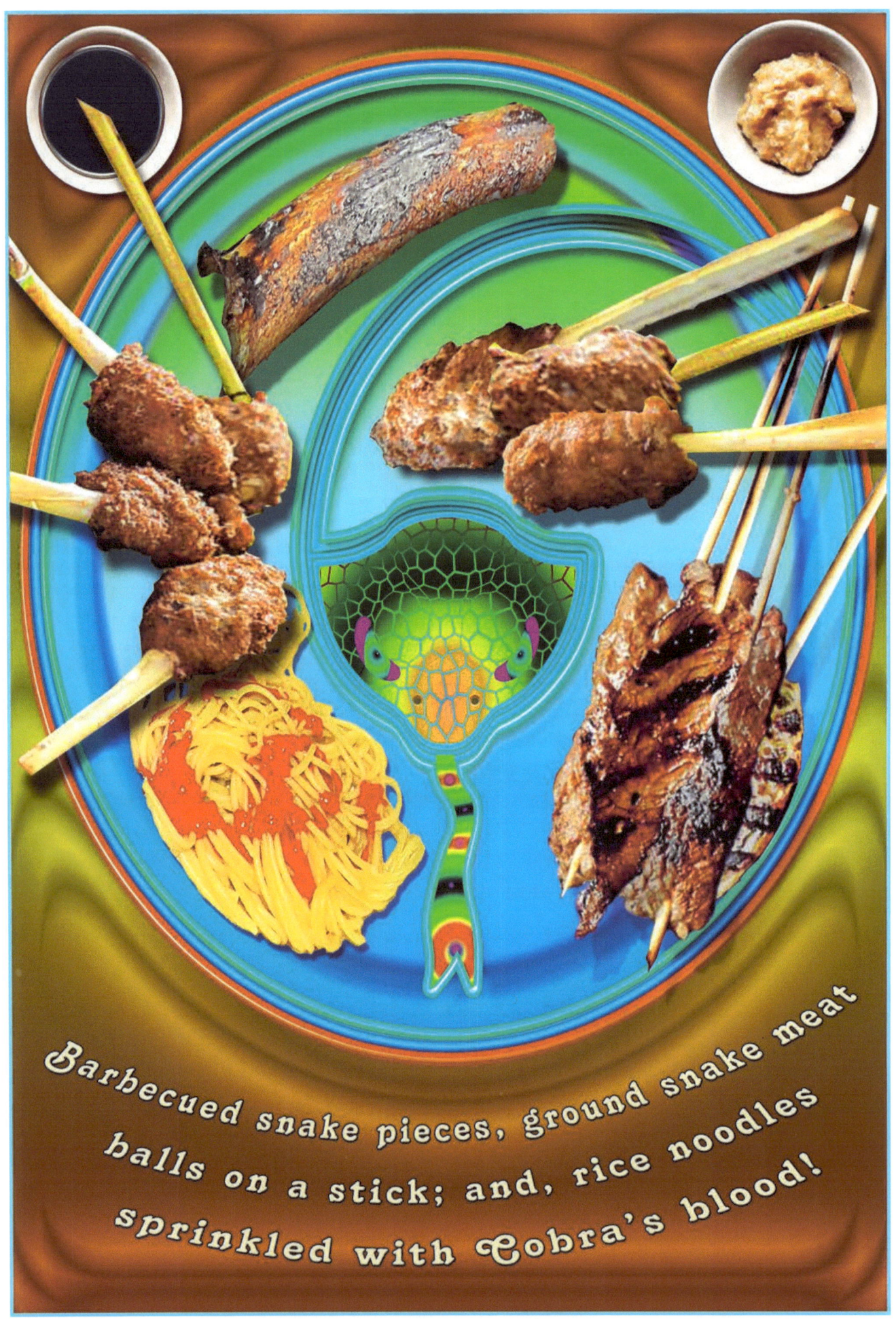

Barbecued snake pieces, ground snake meat balls on a stick; and, rice noodles sprinkled with Cobra's blood!

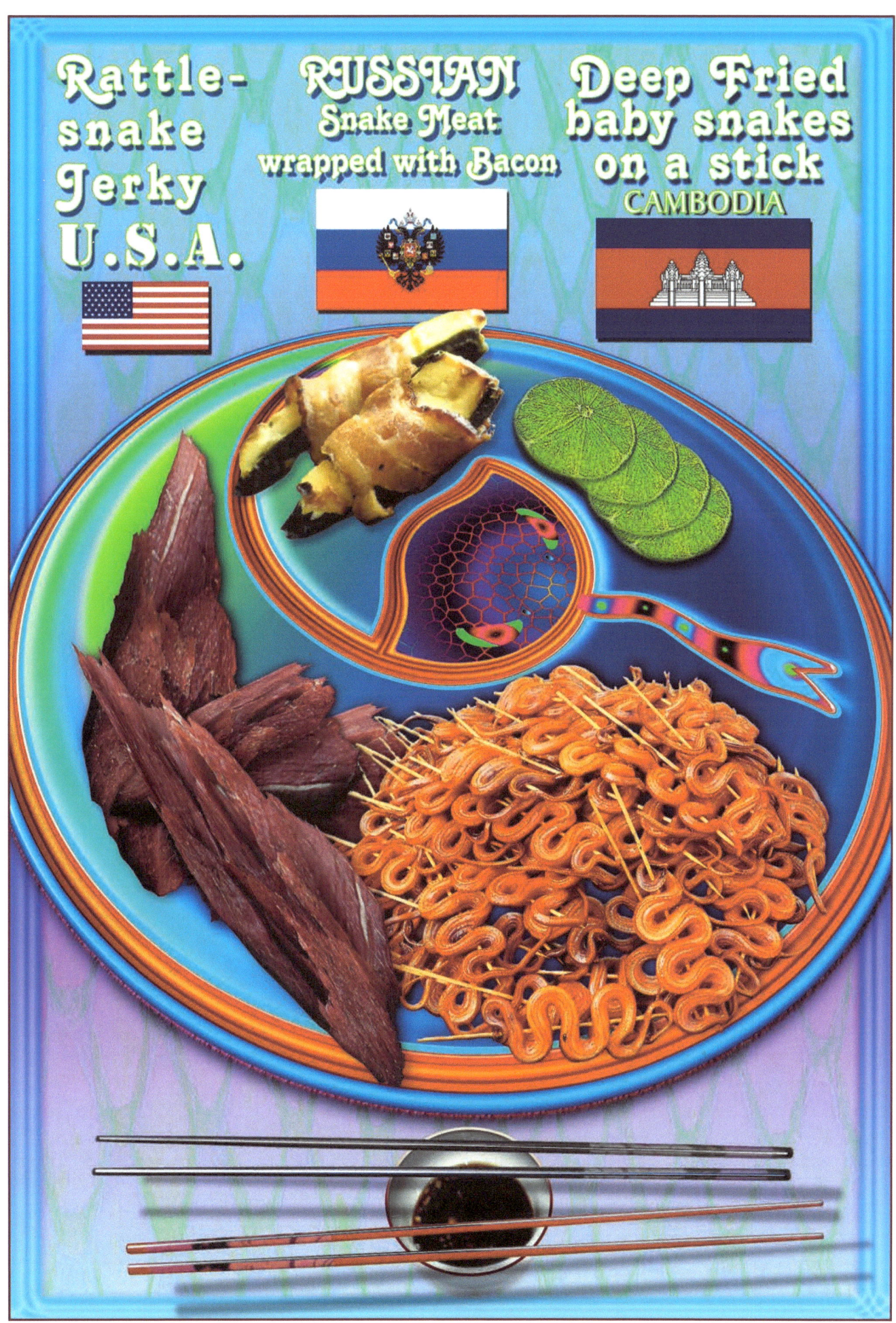

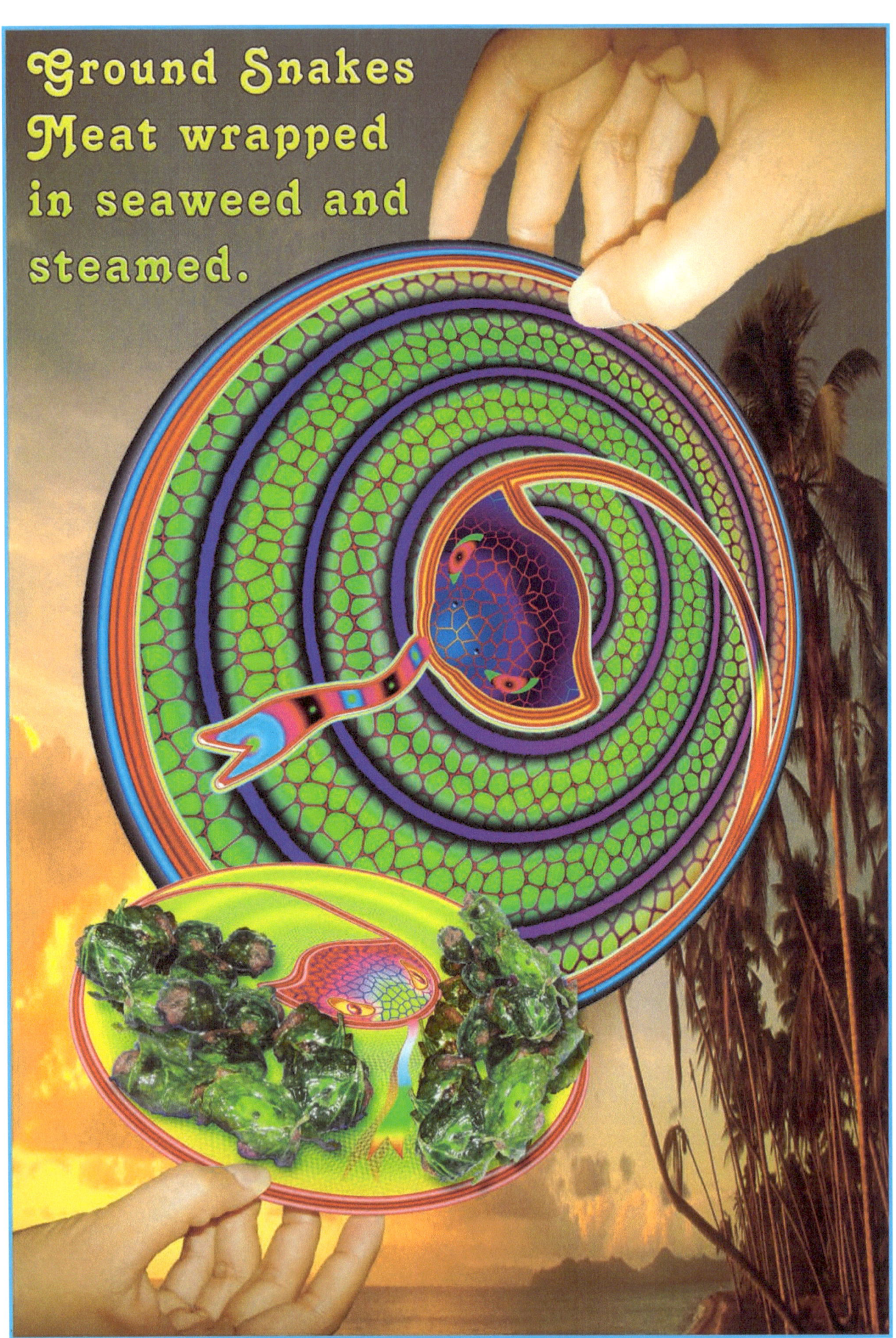

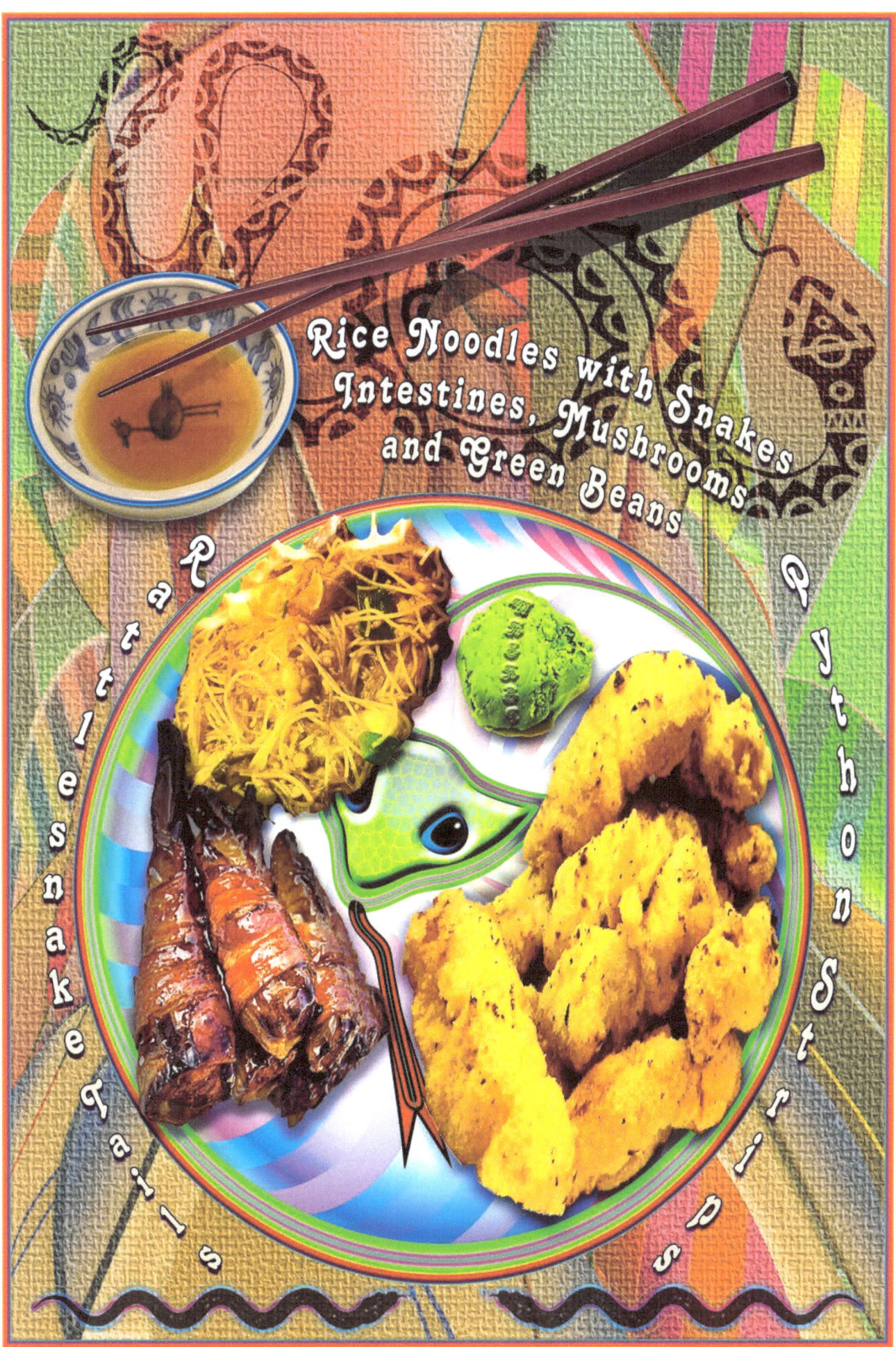

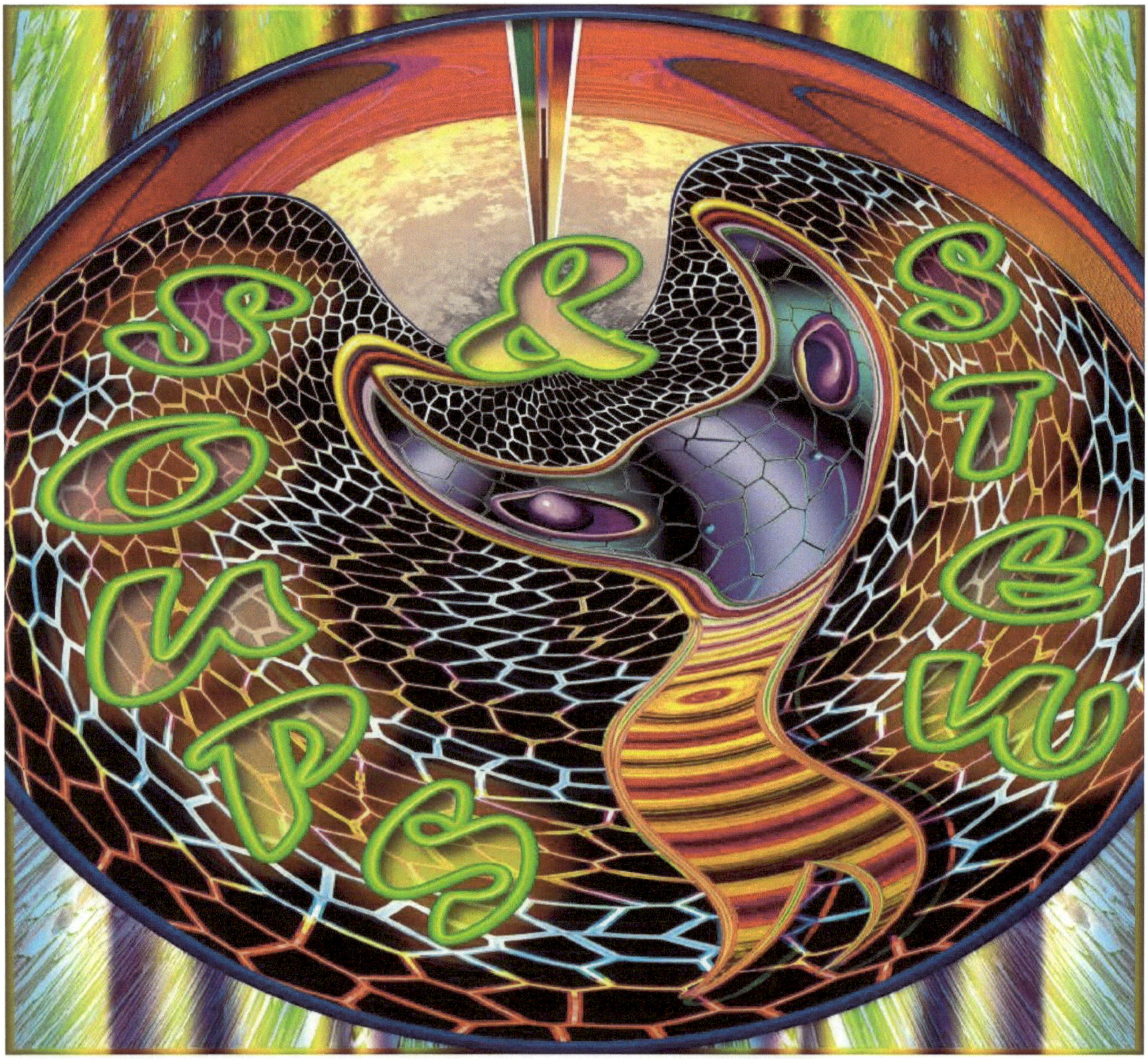

Soups & Stews

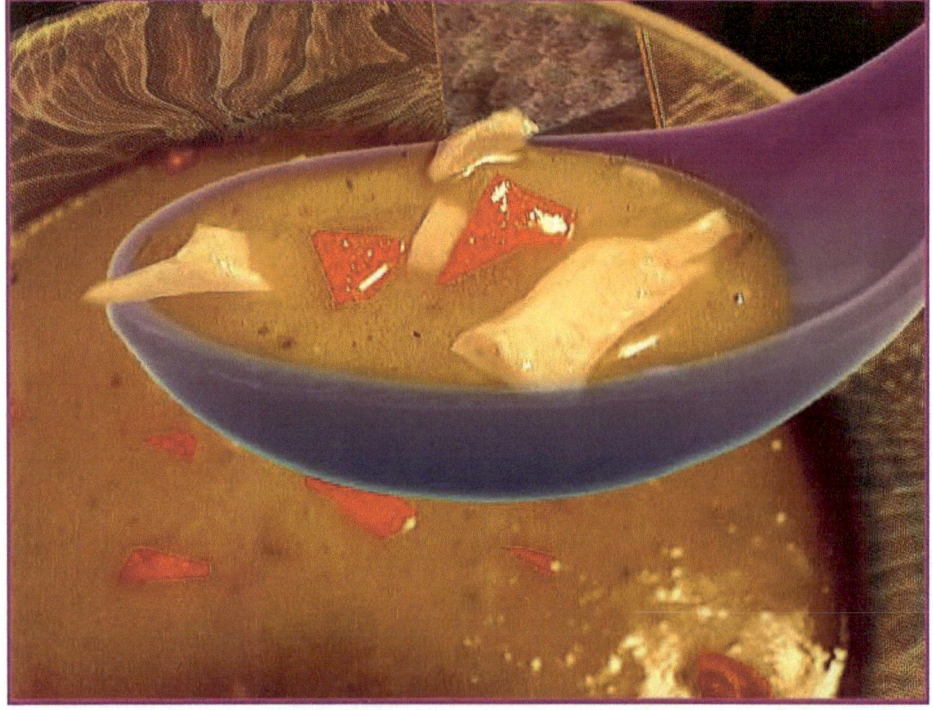

There are several places where snake meat is an essential ingredient for traditional soups and stews; and, depending on availability, there could be as many as five types of snakes used in a single recipe; as well as, a variety of different noodles, vegetables and spices. Some recipes may also include other meats like: pork, fish or chicken.

Left: A popular version of "Thick Broth" Rattlesnake soup.

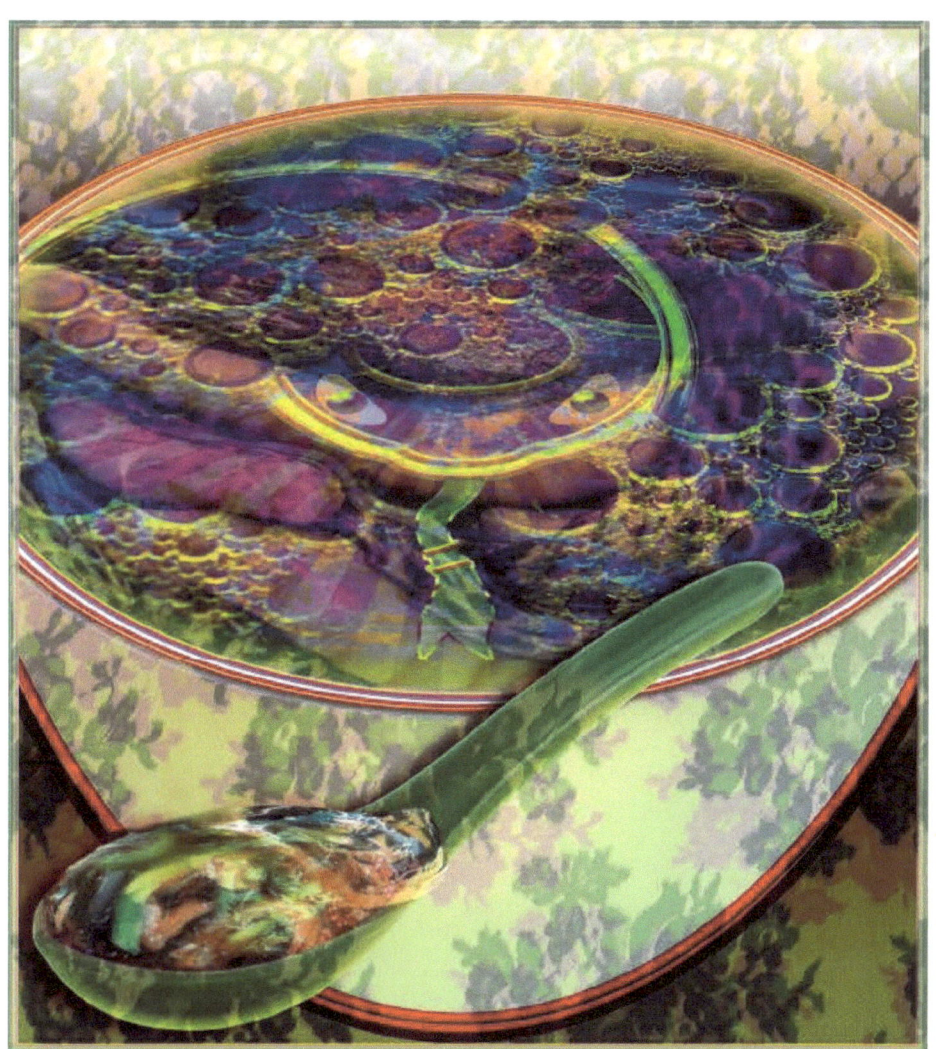

Recipes for Snake Soups and tasty stews have been passed on from generation to generation; with the traditional preparation techniques still practiced, unchanged, to the present day.

Left: Water Snake Soup

Below: cooking snake

Bottom: Poisonous Sea Snake and Mushrooms with breadsticks.

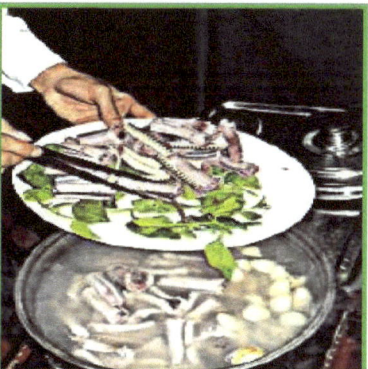

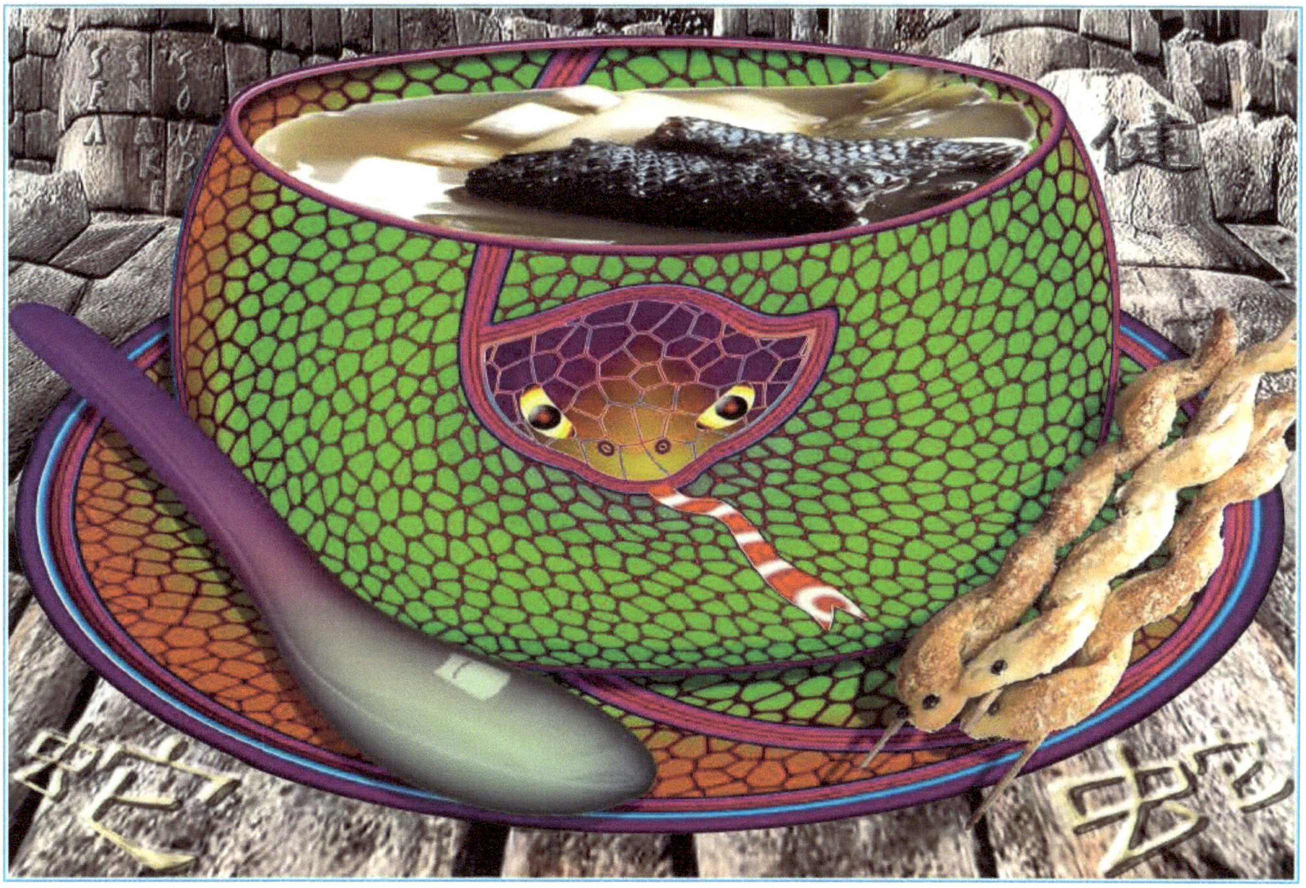

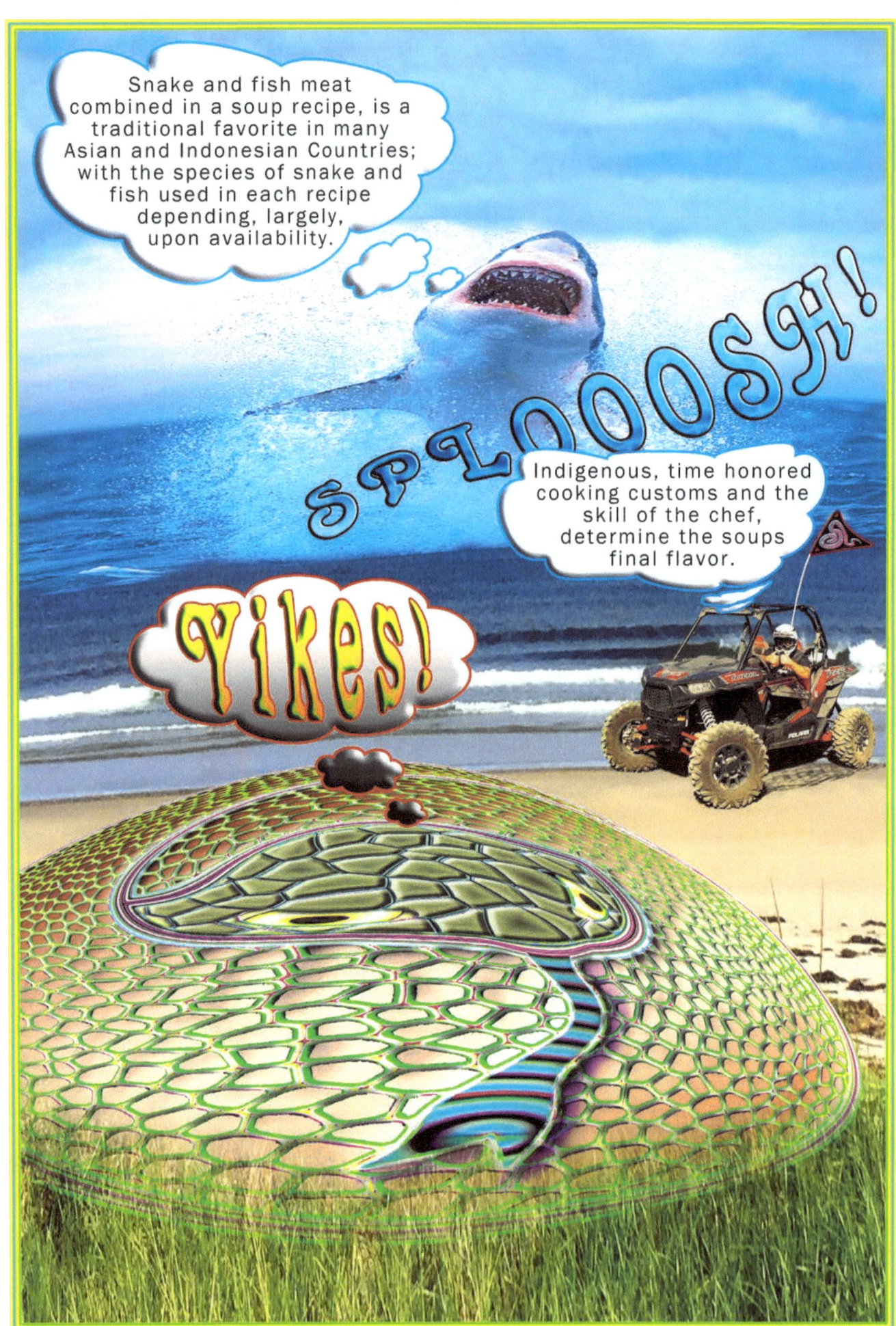

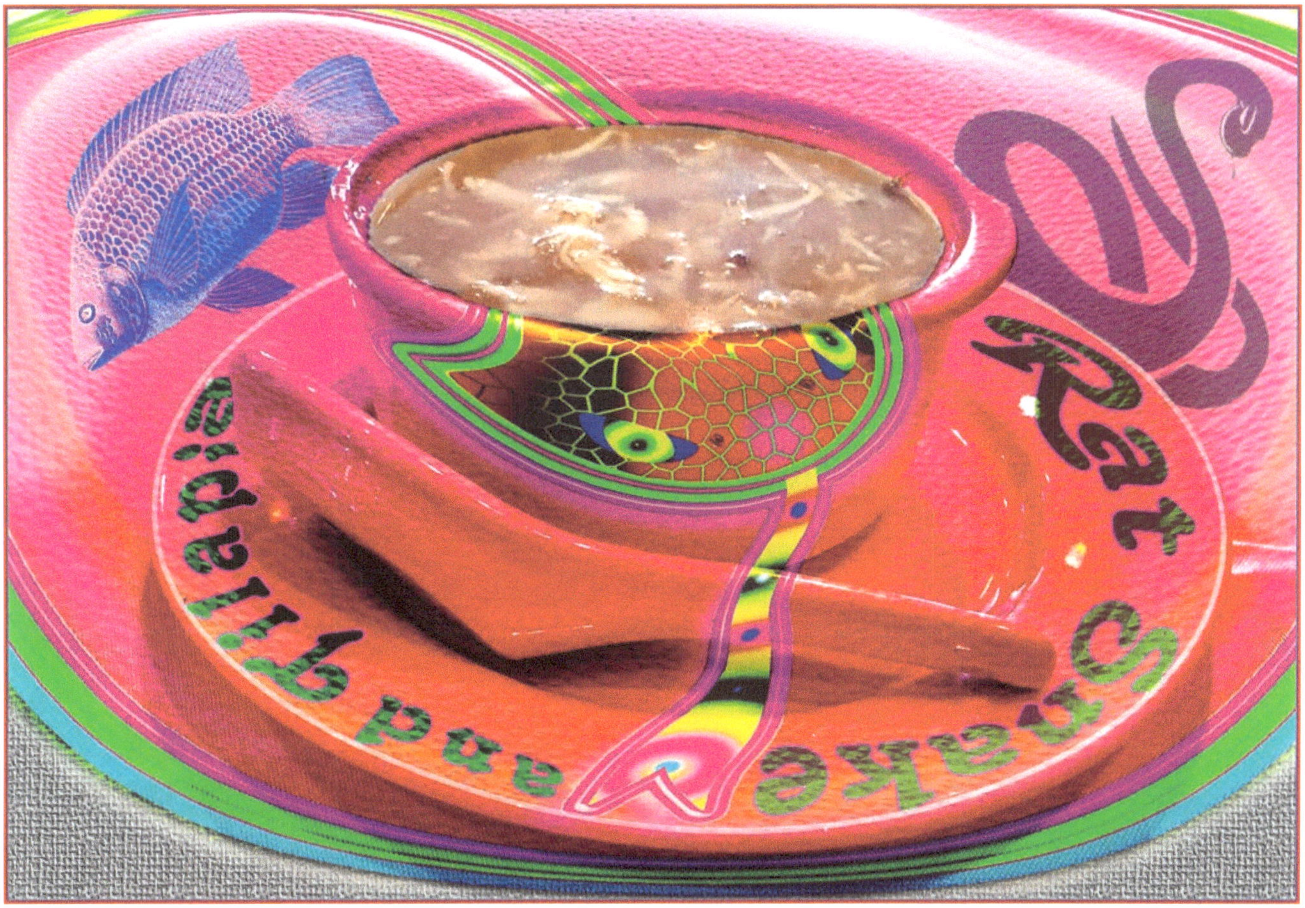

Rat Snake and Giada

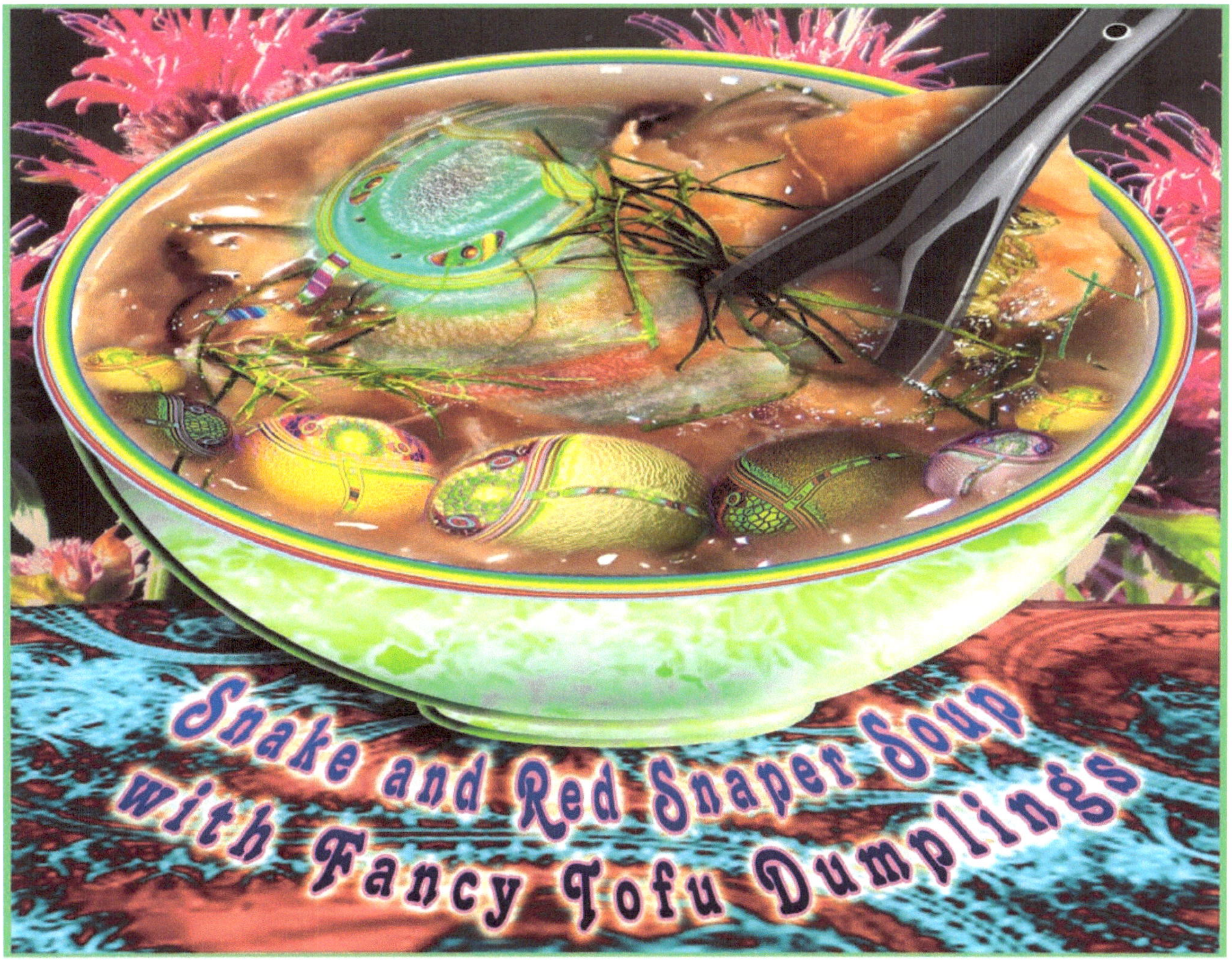

Snake and Red Snaper Soup with Fancy Tofu Dumplings

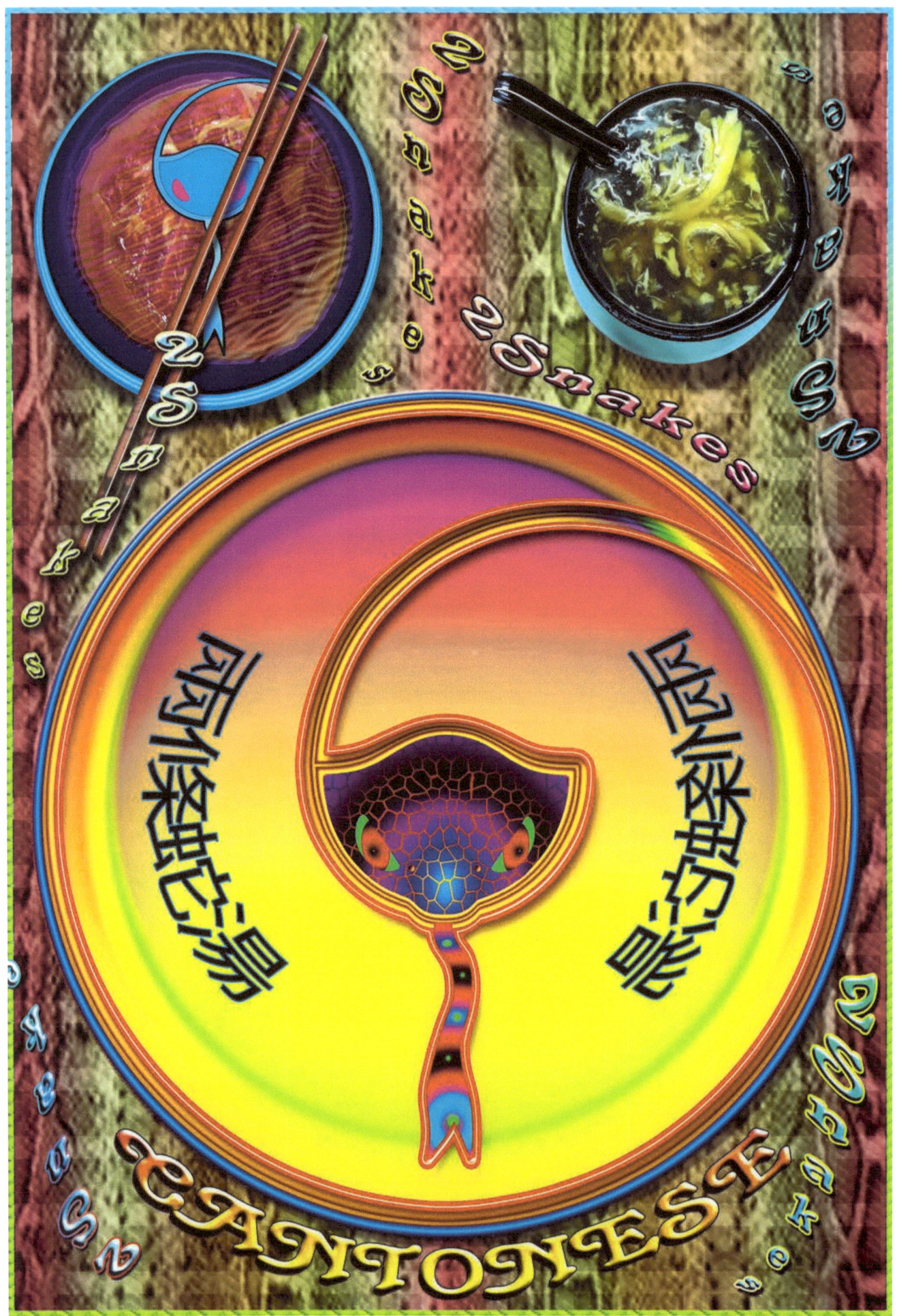

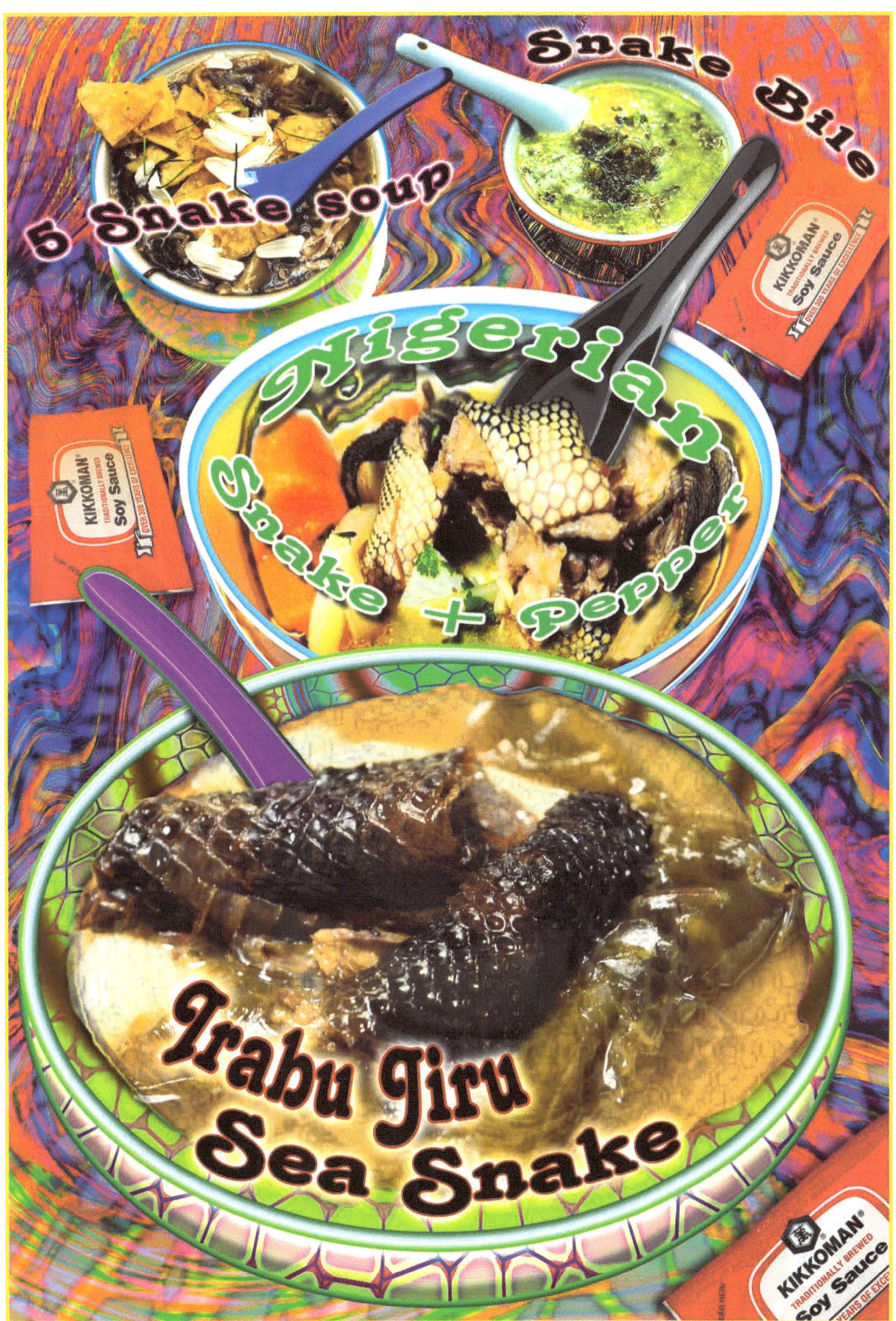

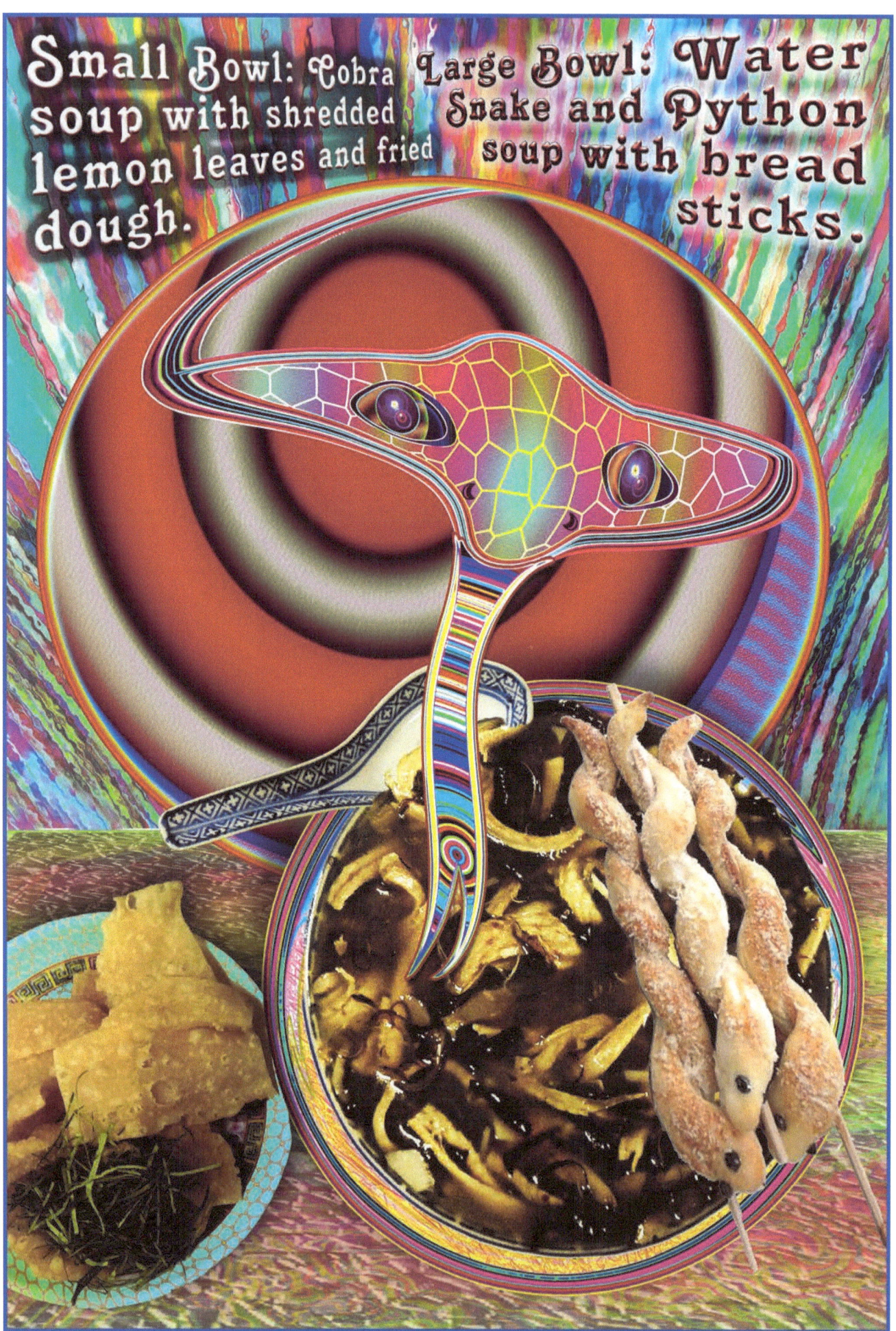

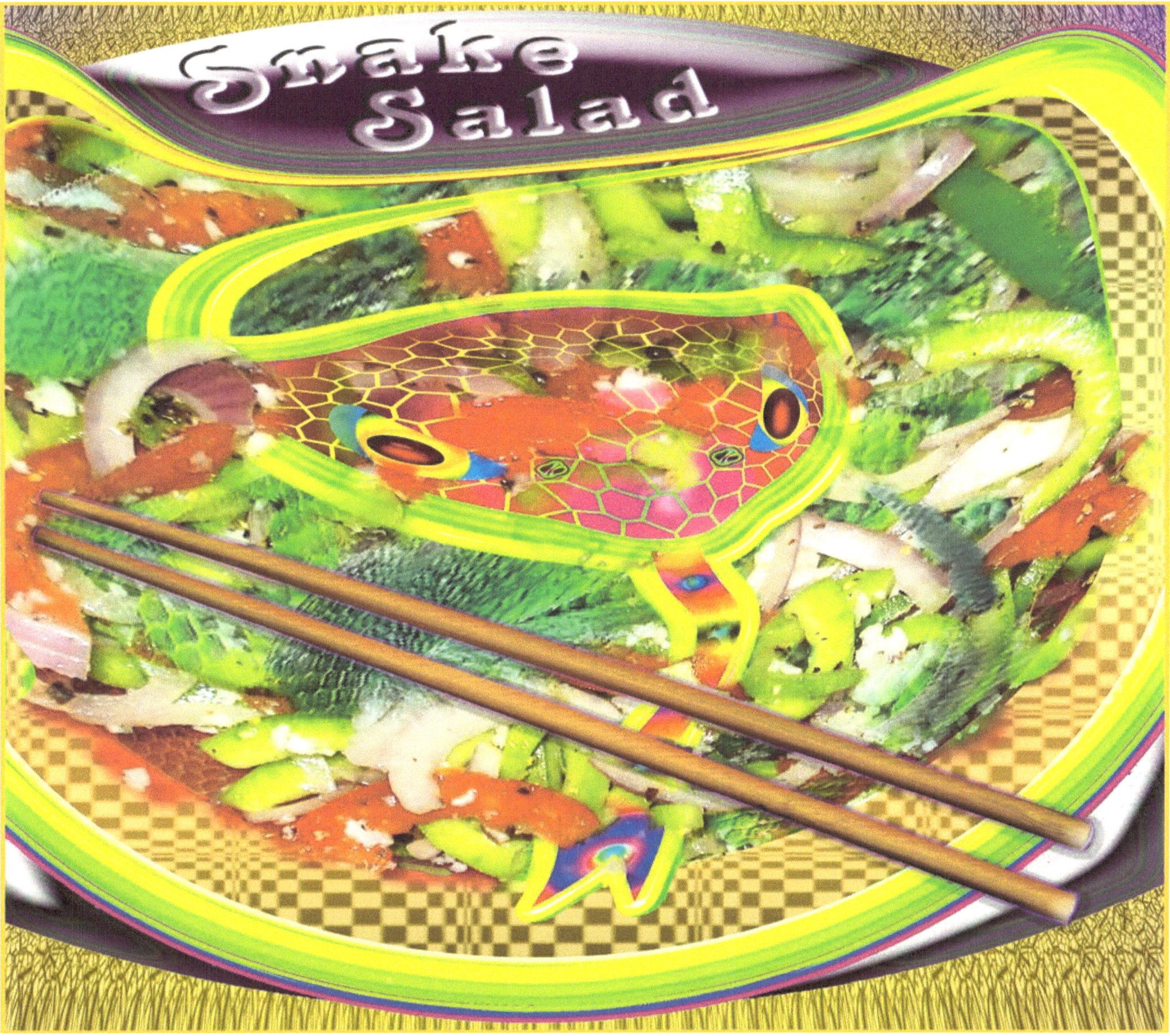

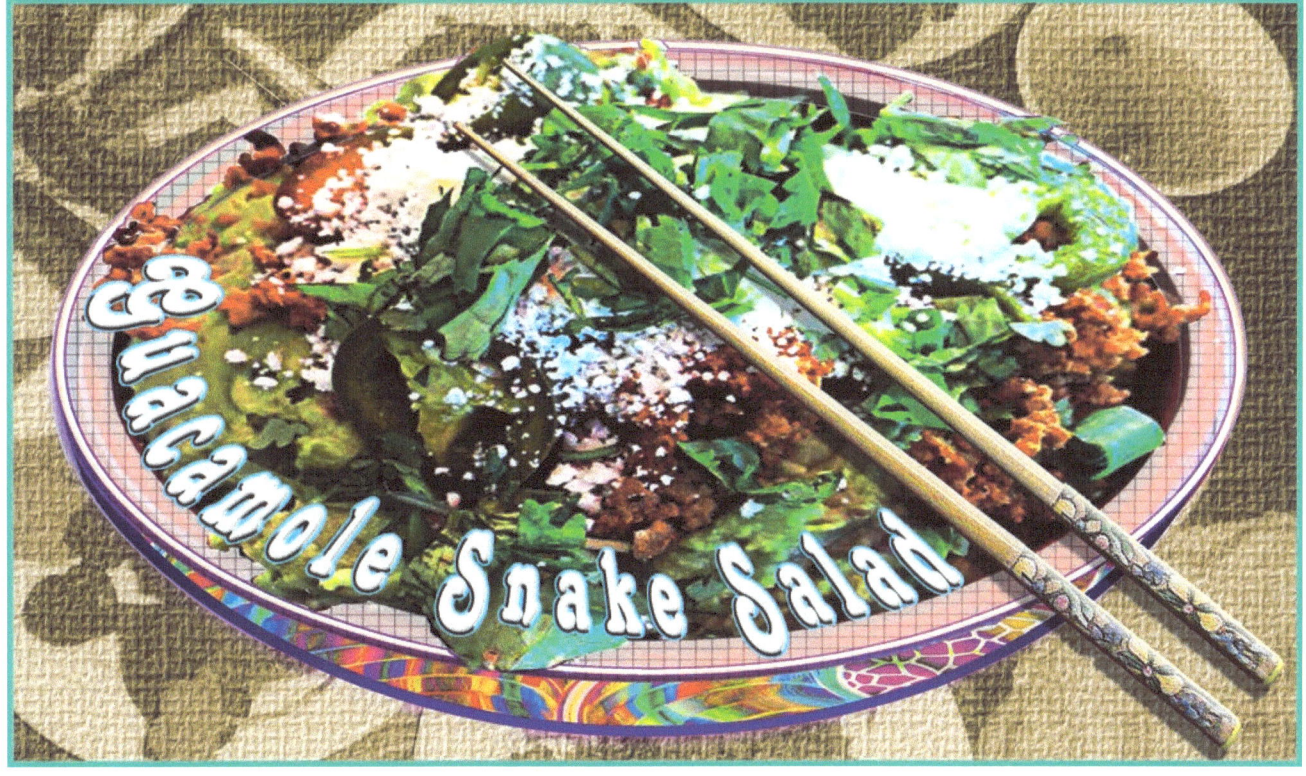

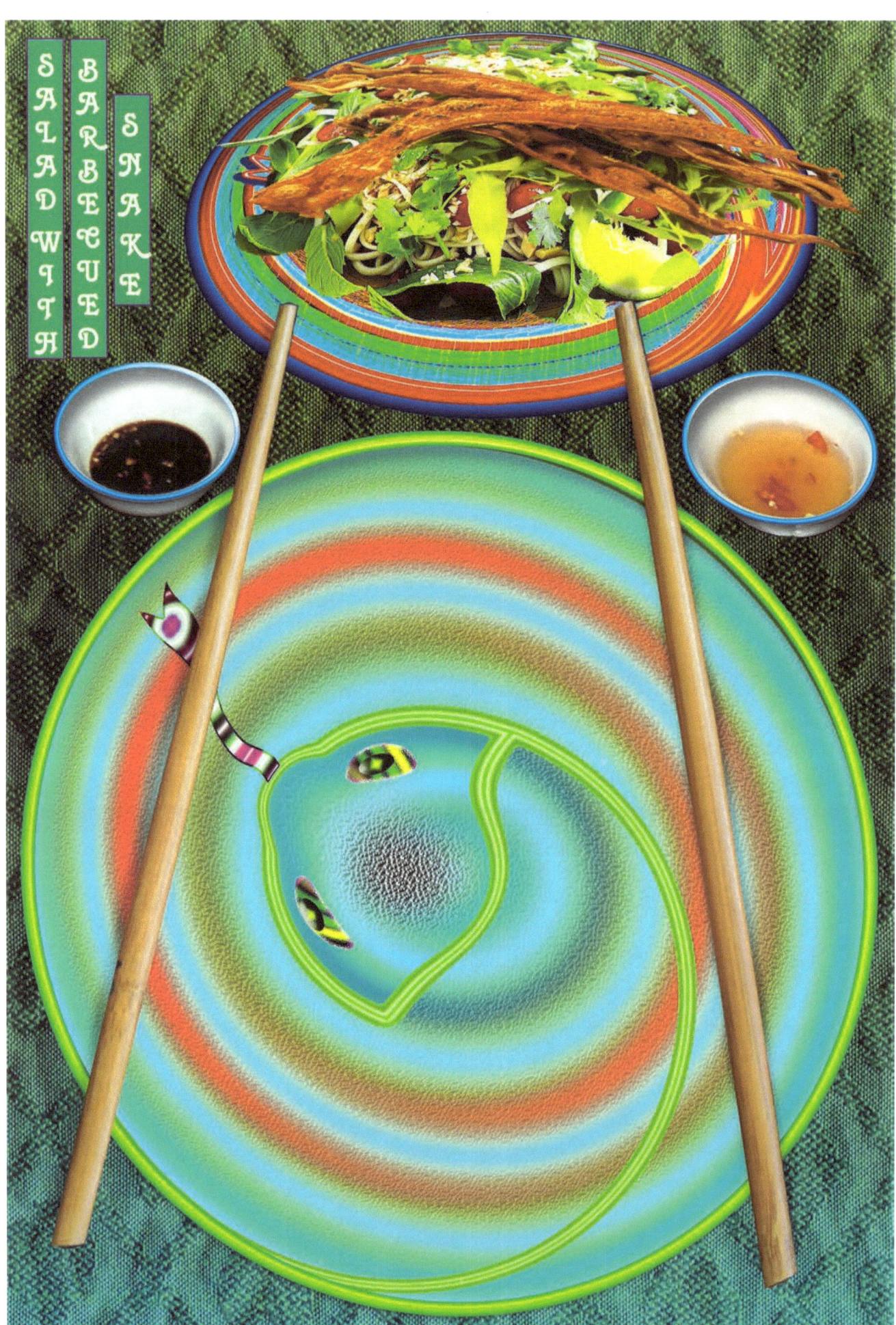

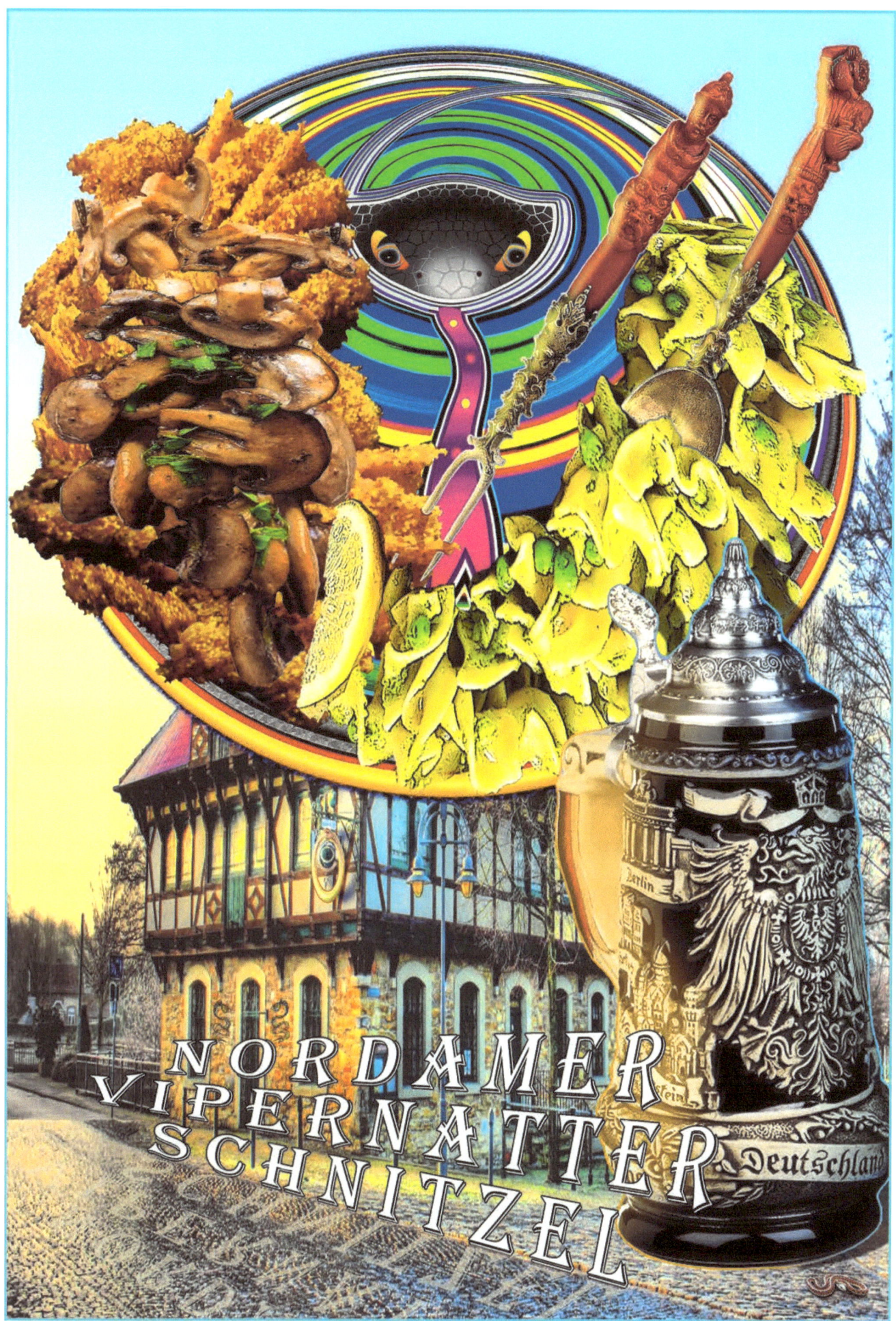

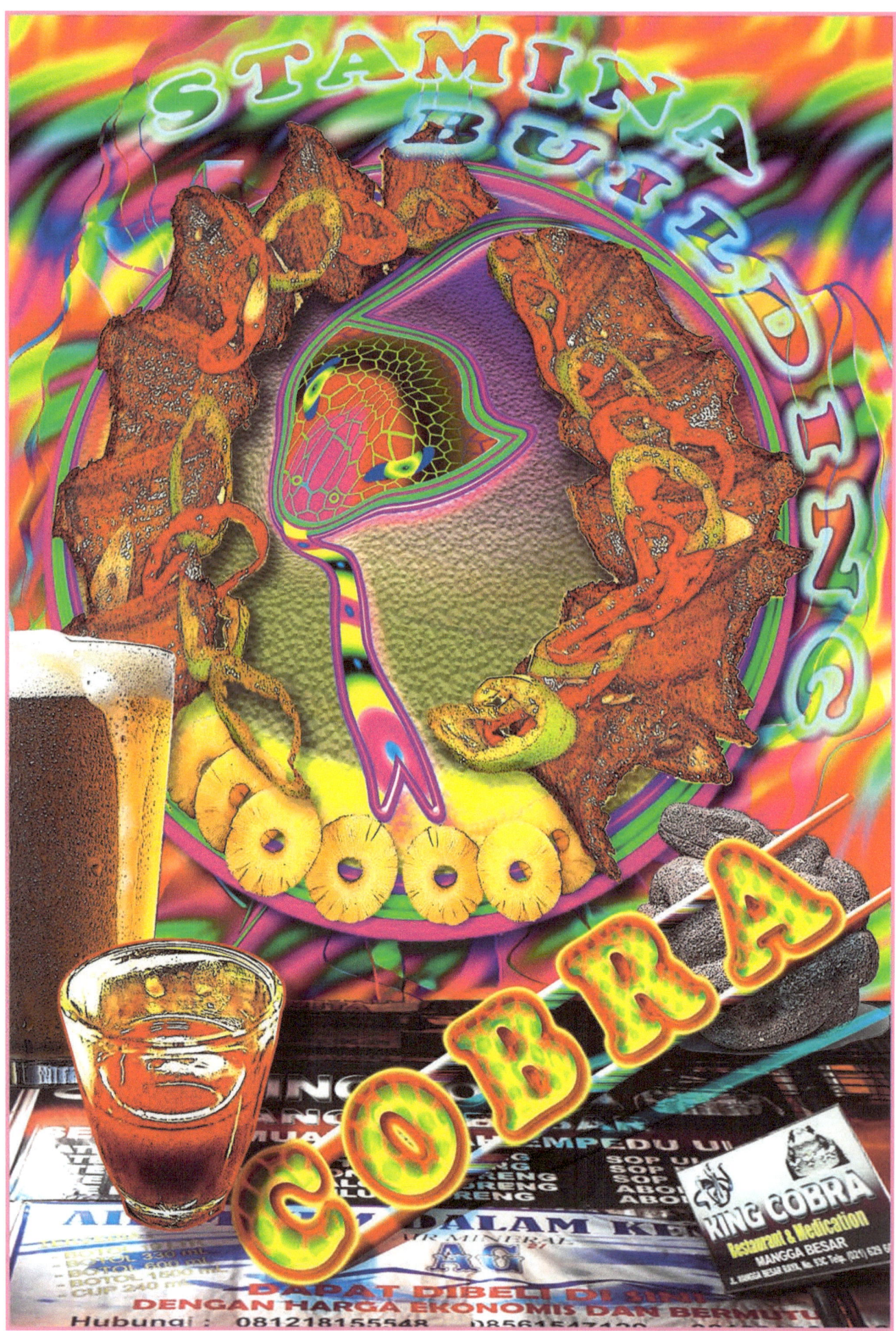

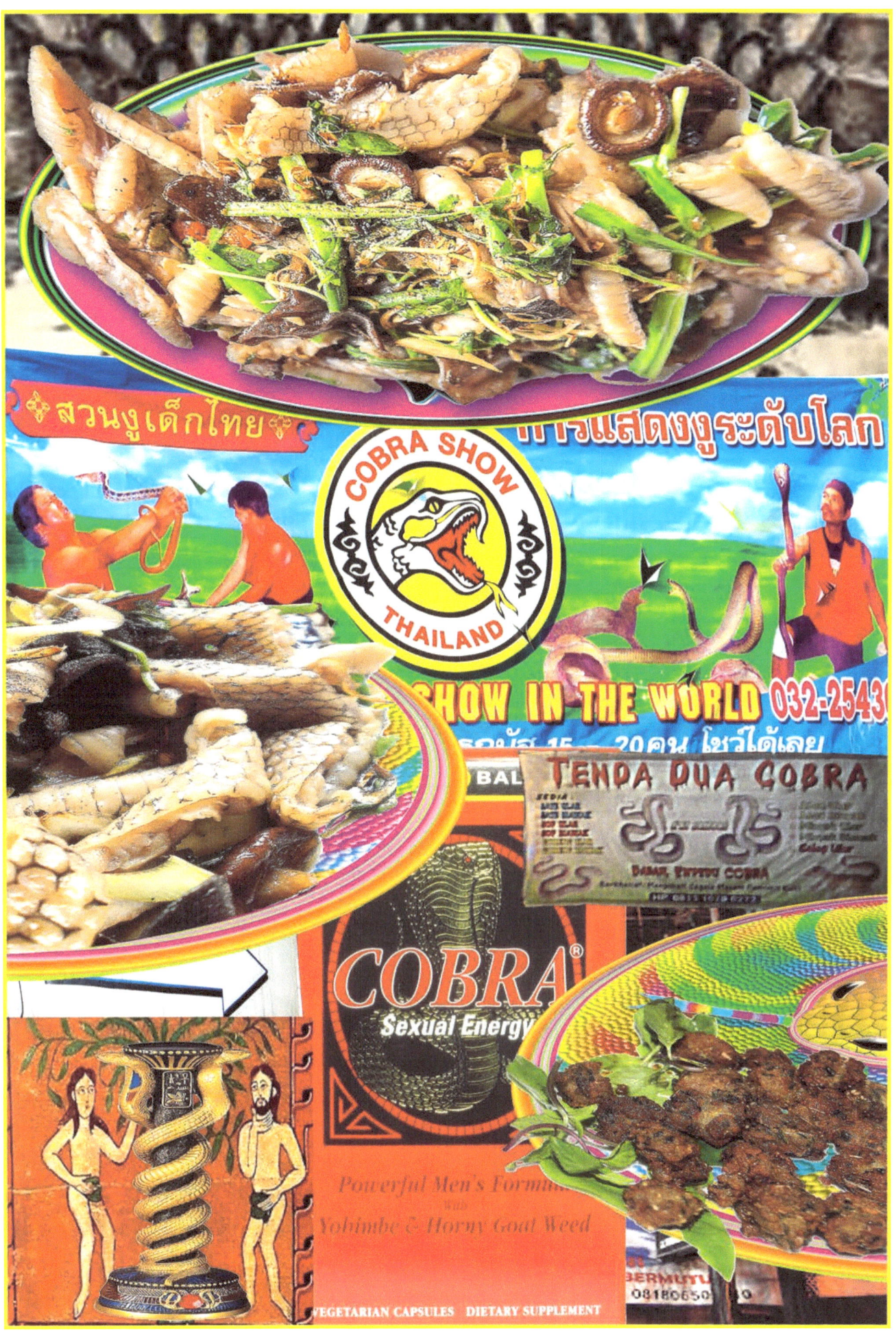

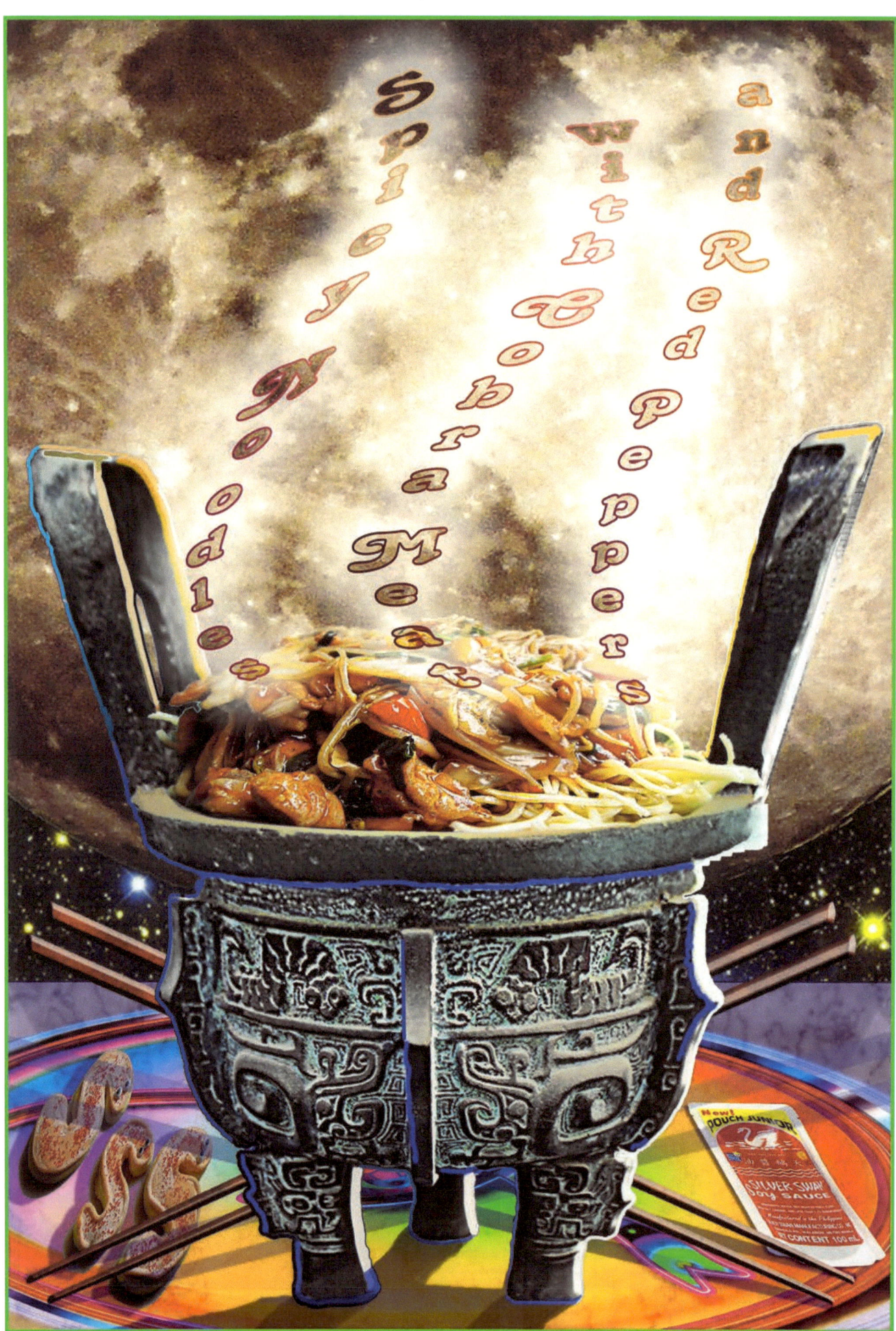

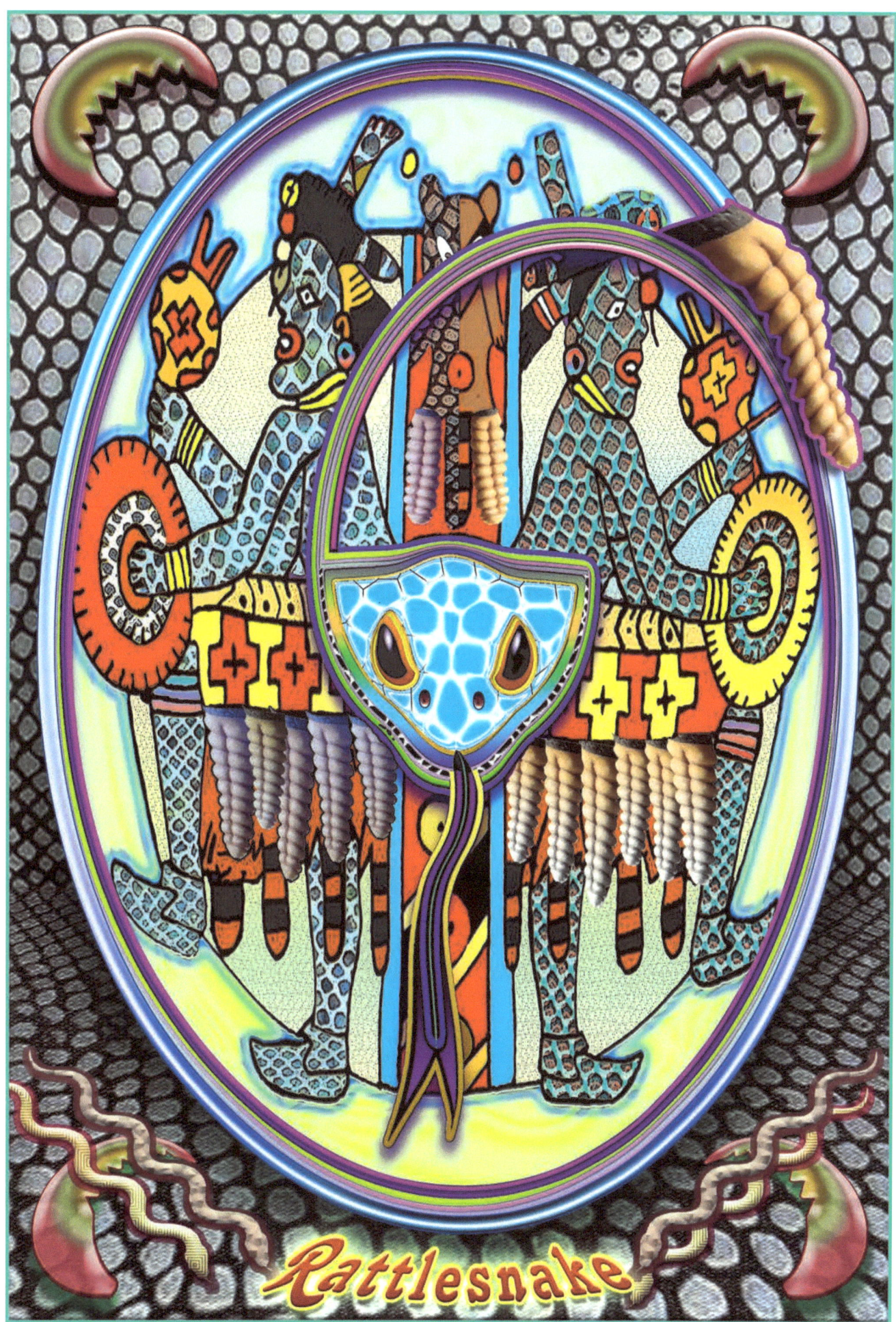

In North and Central America, Mexico and Canada, the snake that's mostly consumed is the Rattlesnake; which, includes some 32 different species and 82 subspecies. The ancient **Mayans** believed that the rattlesnake was a link to the "other world" and called these snakes a "vision serpent." Rattlesnakes also had a key role in **Aztec** mythology. In the Aztec religion, **Xiuhcoatl** was a mythological serpent, and was regarded as the spirit form of X I U H T E C U H T L I, the Aztec fire deity, and was also an **atlatl** wielded by **Huitzilopochtli**.

Most rattlesnake species are not classified as endangered, according to the **IUCN (International Union for the Conservation of Nature.)** *The Aruba Island rattlesnake is considered critically endangered, and there are three other species on the Red List of Threatened Species: Santa Catalina Island rattlesnake: Critically endangered due to its limited range. Human and feral cat killings are two of the biggest threats to this species of snake. The Tancitaran dusky rattlesnake: Considered endangered because It's only found in one small area of Mexico.*

Below: Rattlesnake dipped in beer batter and breaded, roasted corn on the cob, "Rattler" with vegetables soup, and mayonnaise as a "dipping" condiment.

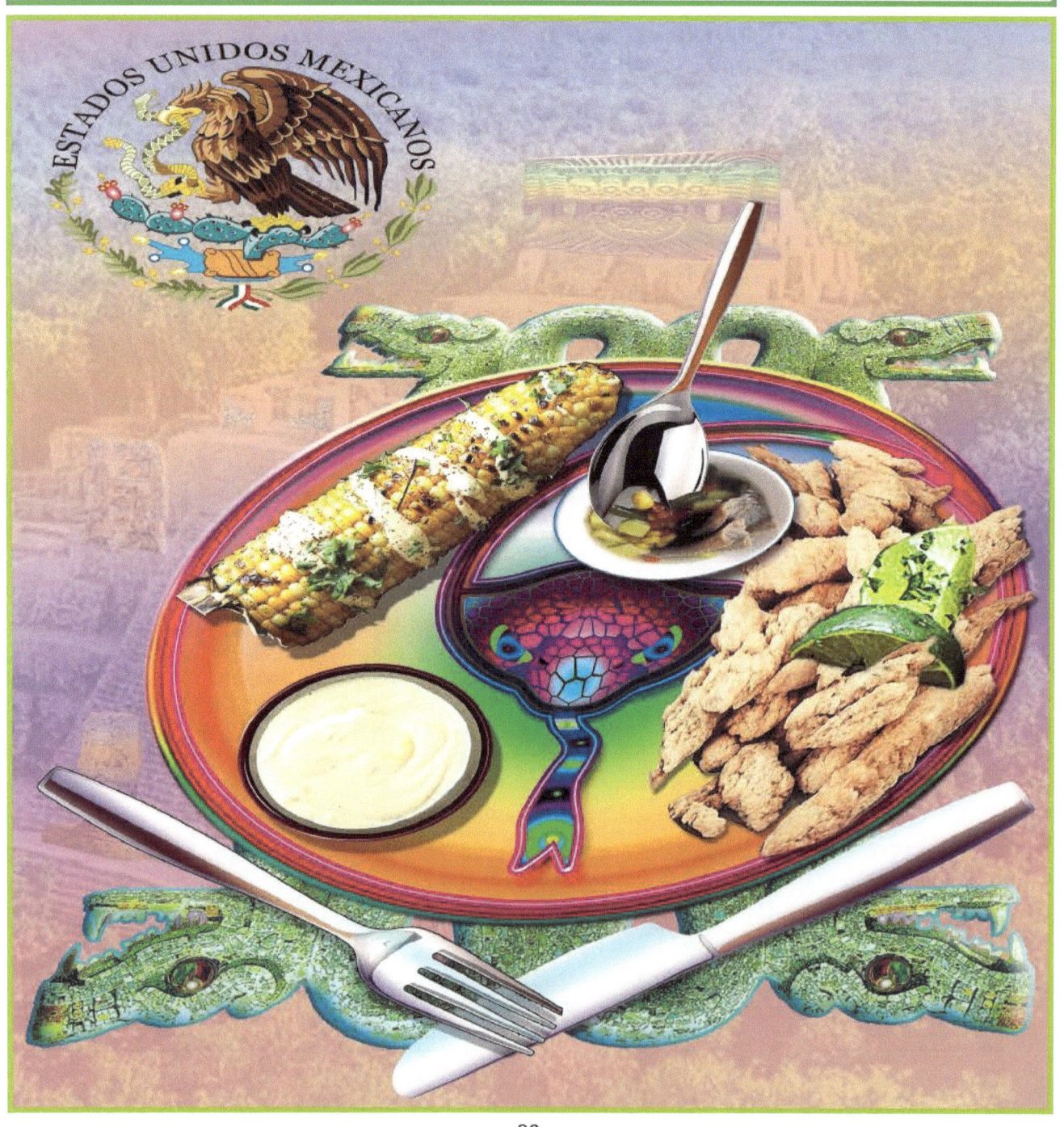

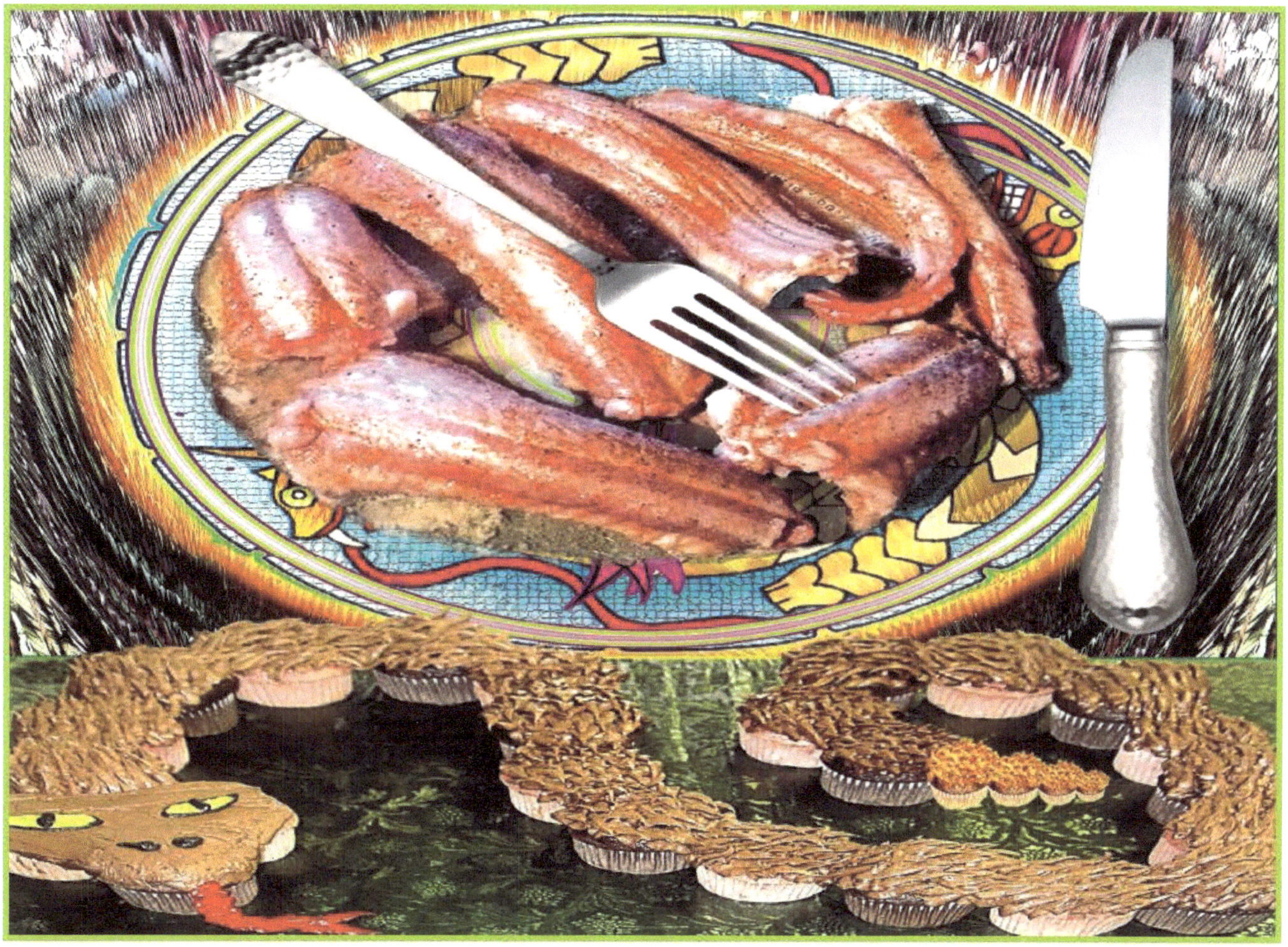

Above: Skillet-Fried, Free Range Rattlesnake with a cleverly made "Rattler" made of chocolate and vanilla cup-cakes for desert. **Below:** Breaded, and deep fried "rattlesnake", roasted corn on the cob with leeks, French fries and "snaky" bread.

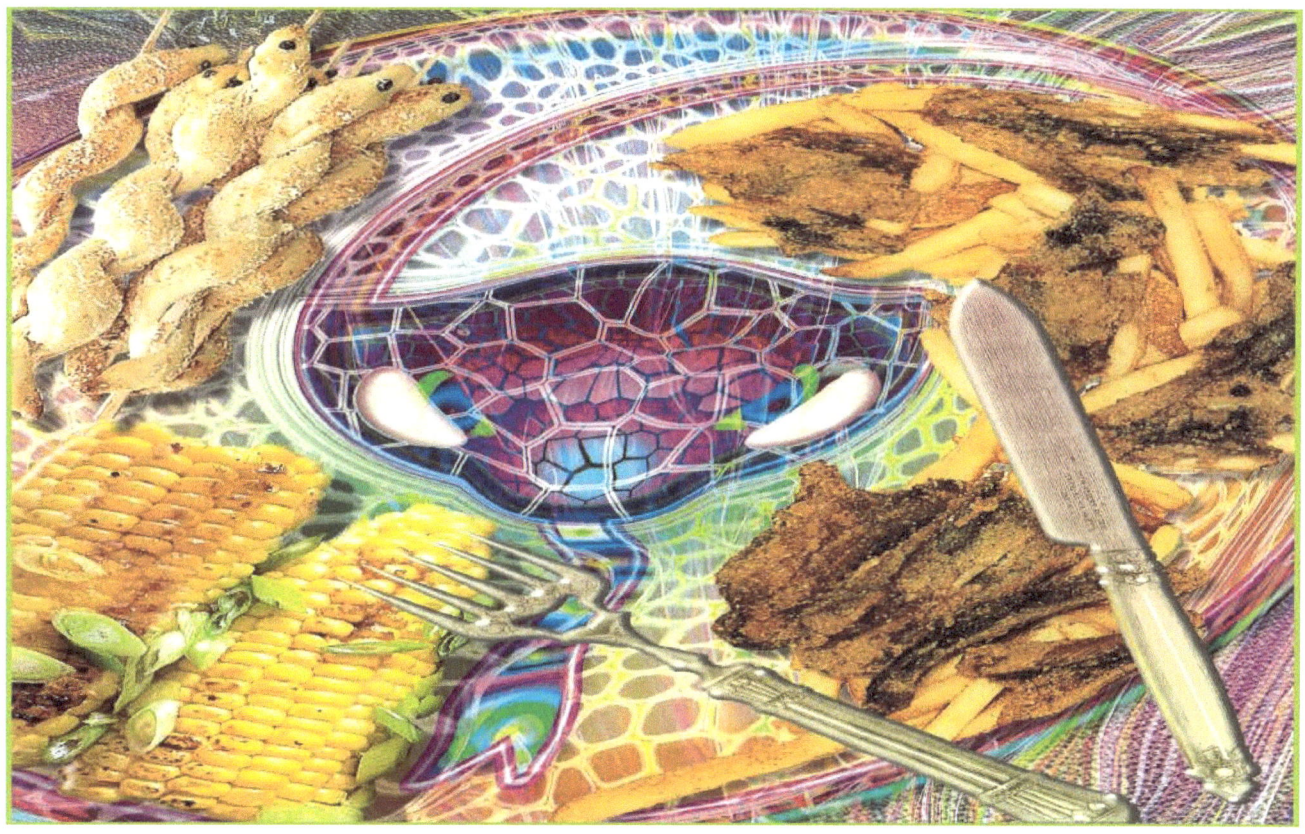

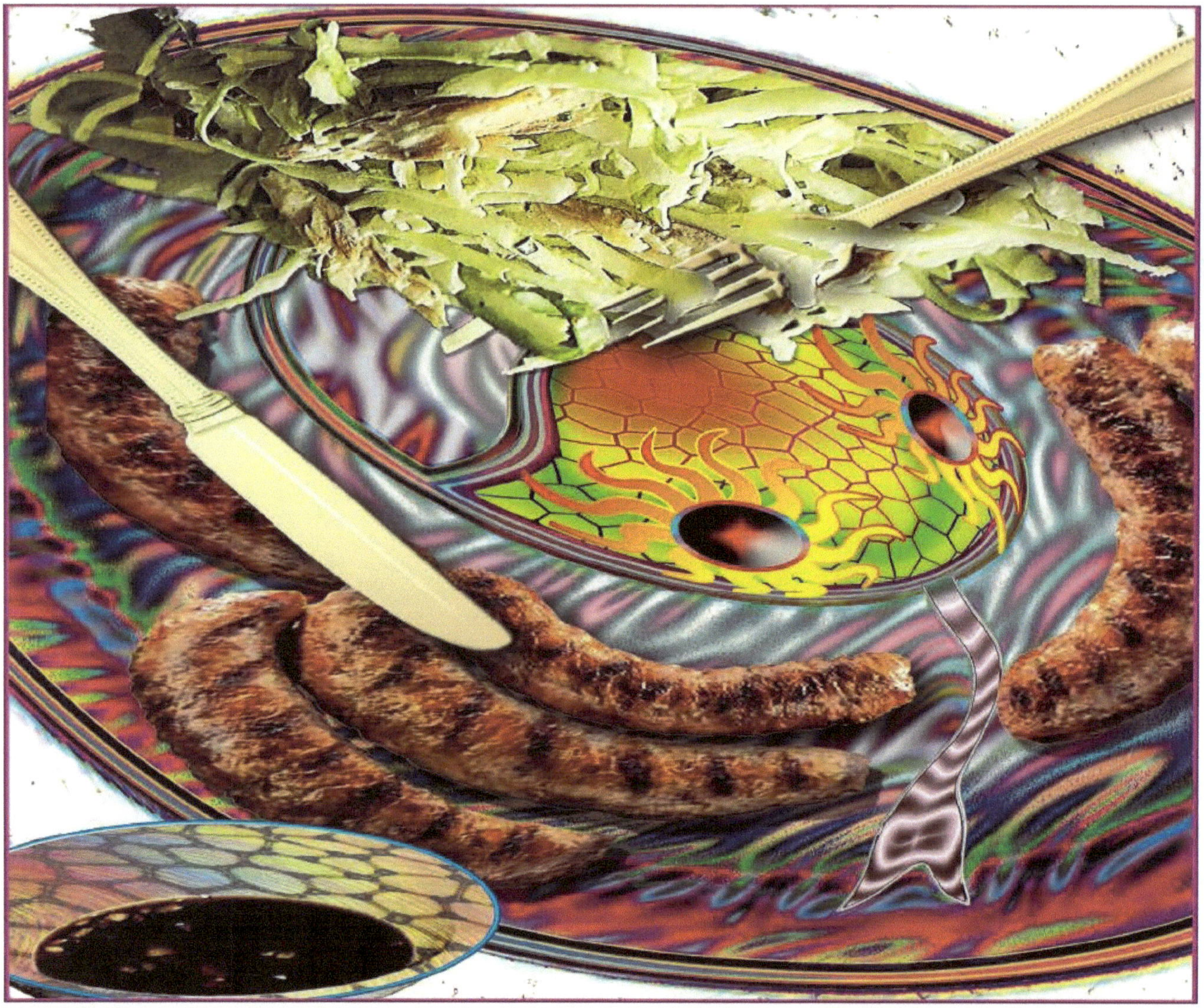

There are several variations of Rattlesnake sausage; from straight "Rattler", to blends with other meats like: rabbit, pheasant, pork, beef and Buffalo. Above: Rattlesnake and Rabbit, Jalapeno sausage with coleslaw.

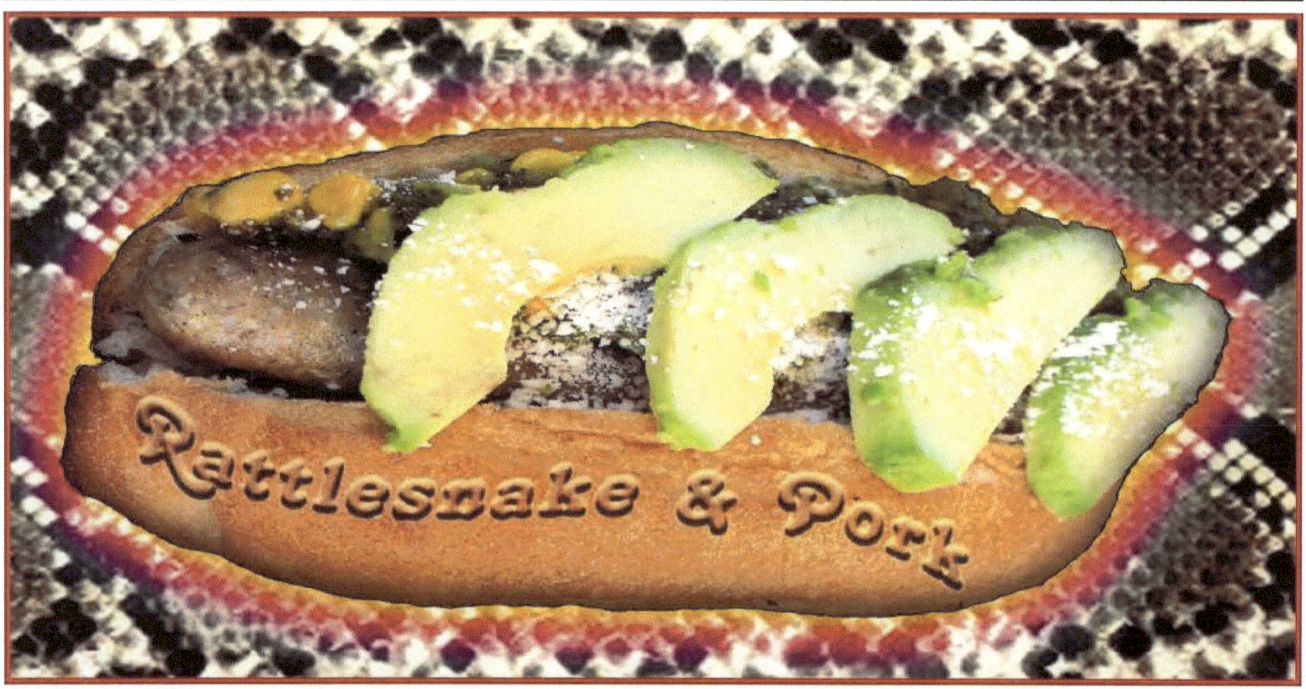

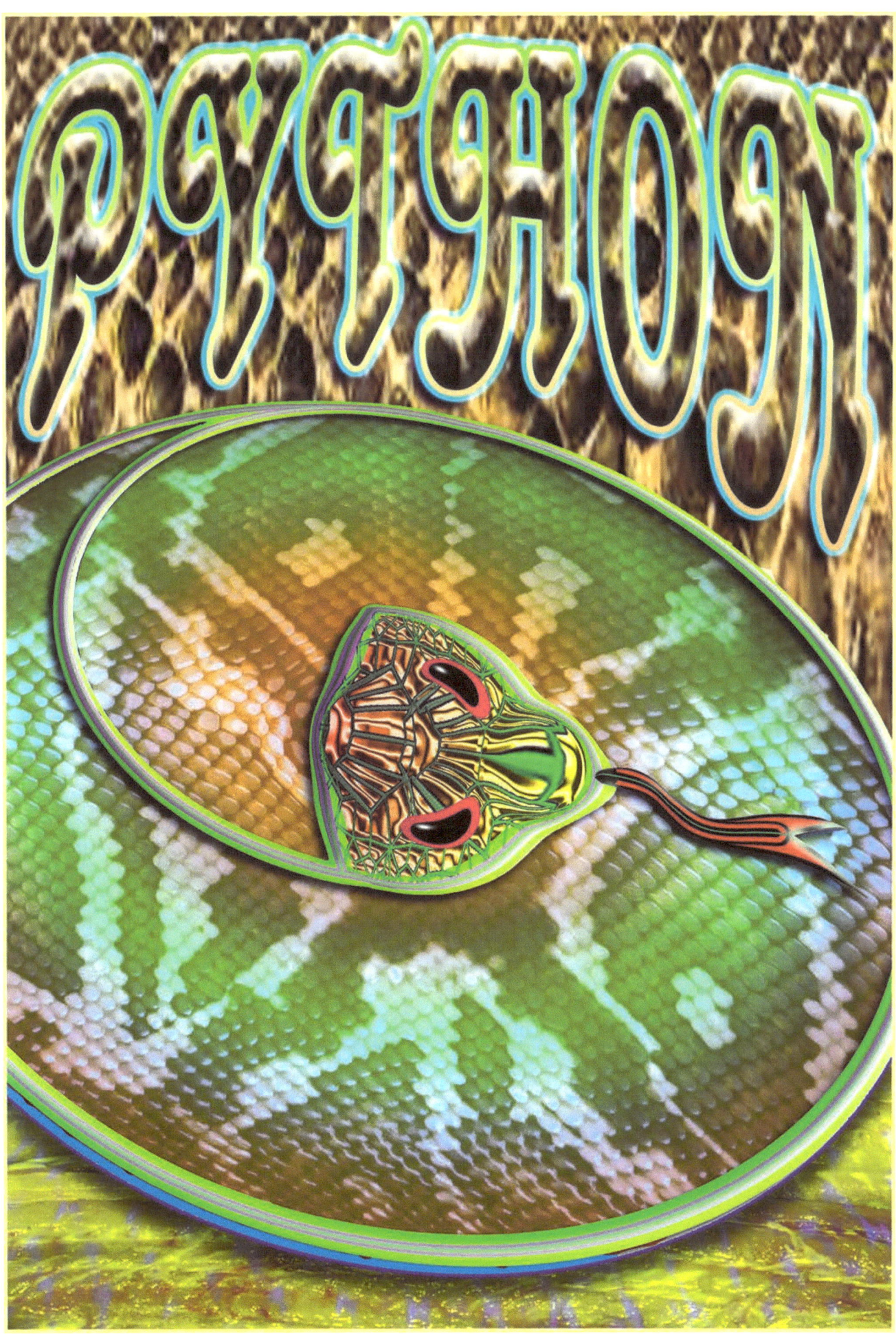

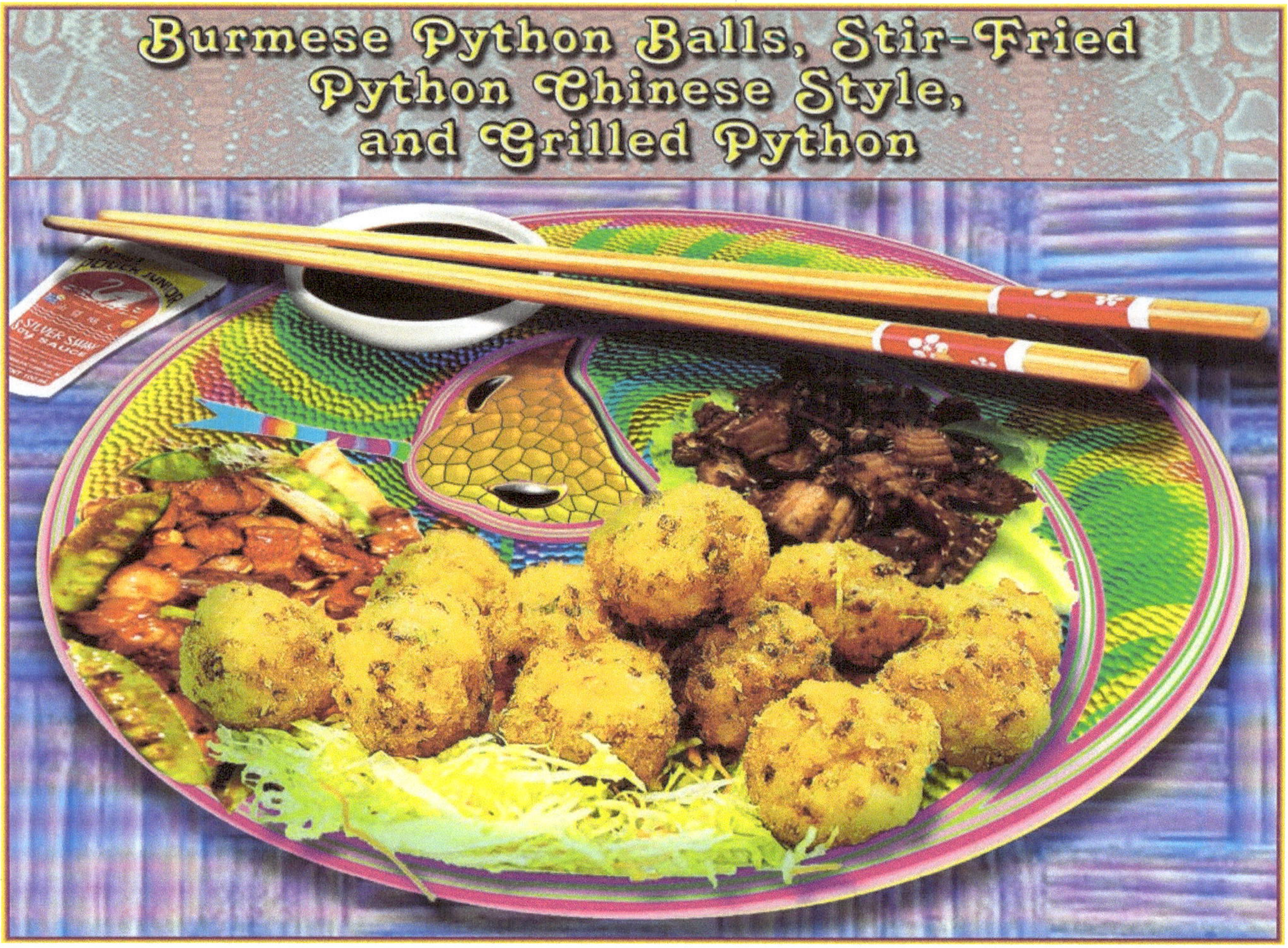

Burmese Python Balls, Stir-Fried Python Chinese Style, and Grilled Python

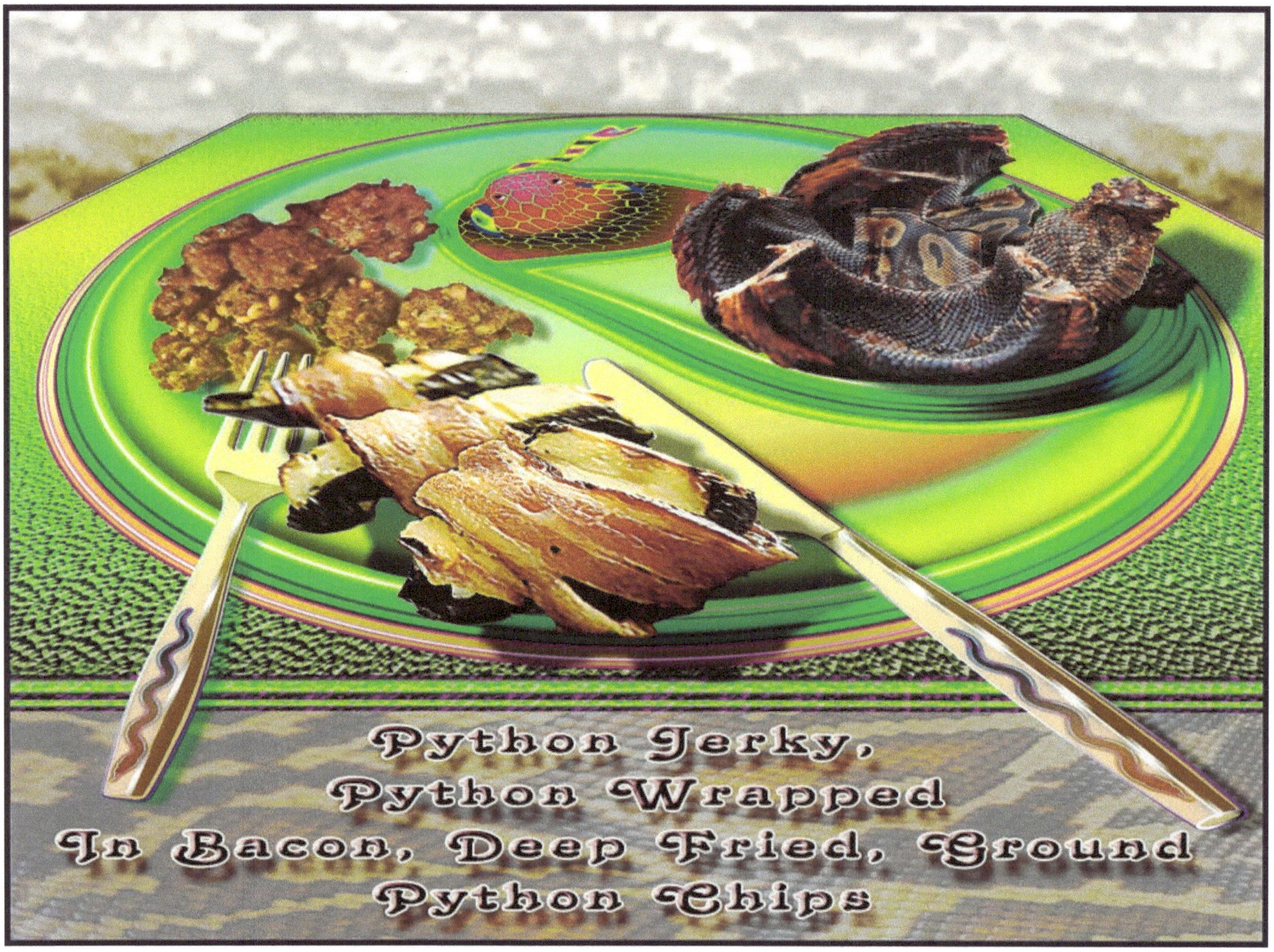

Python Jerky, Python Wrapped In Bacon, Deep Fried, Ground Python Chips

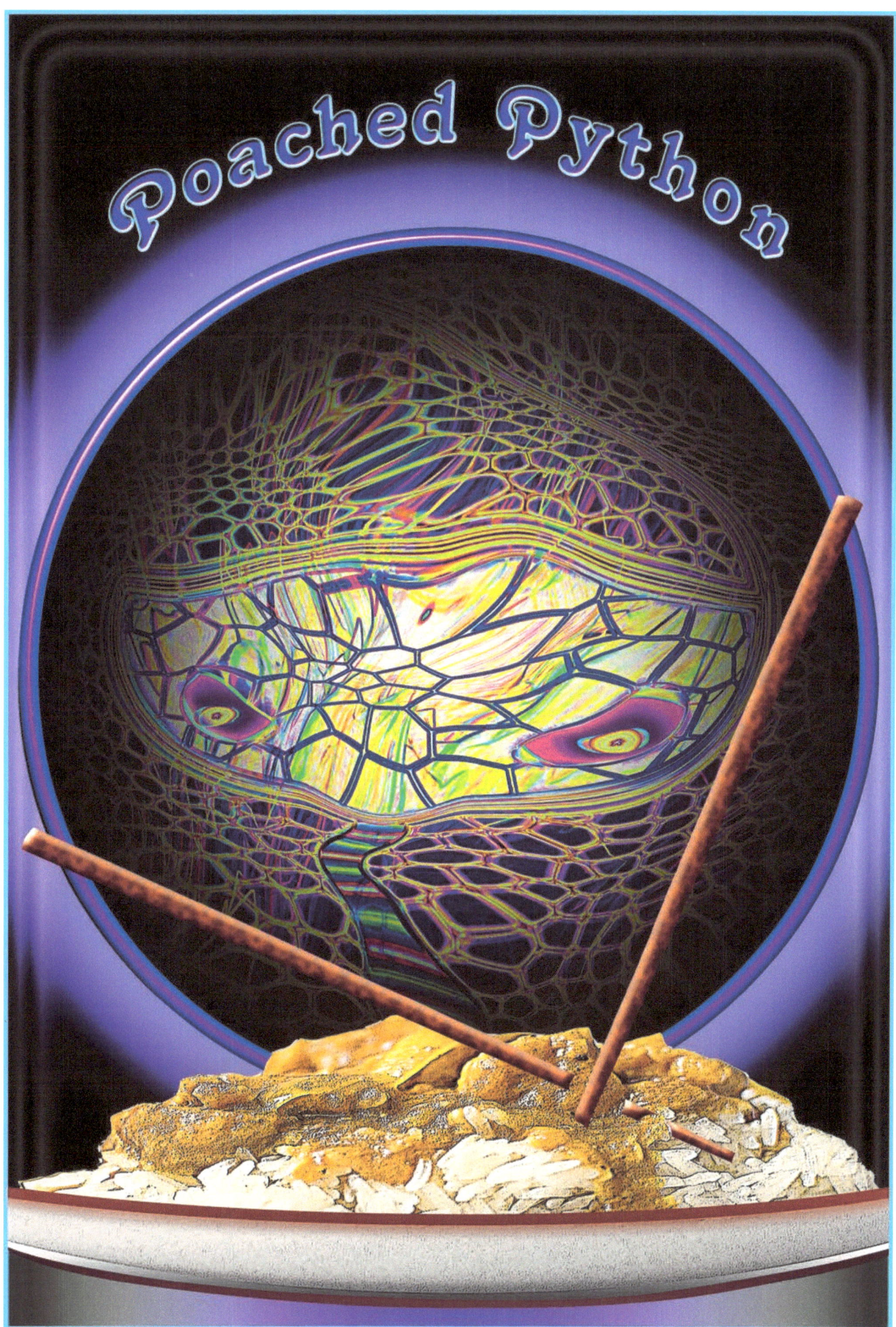

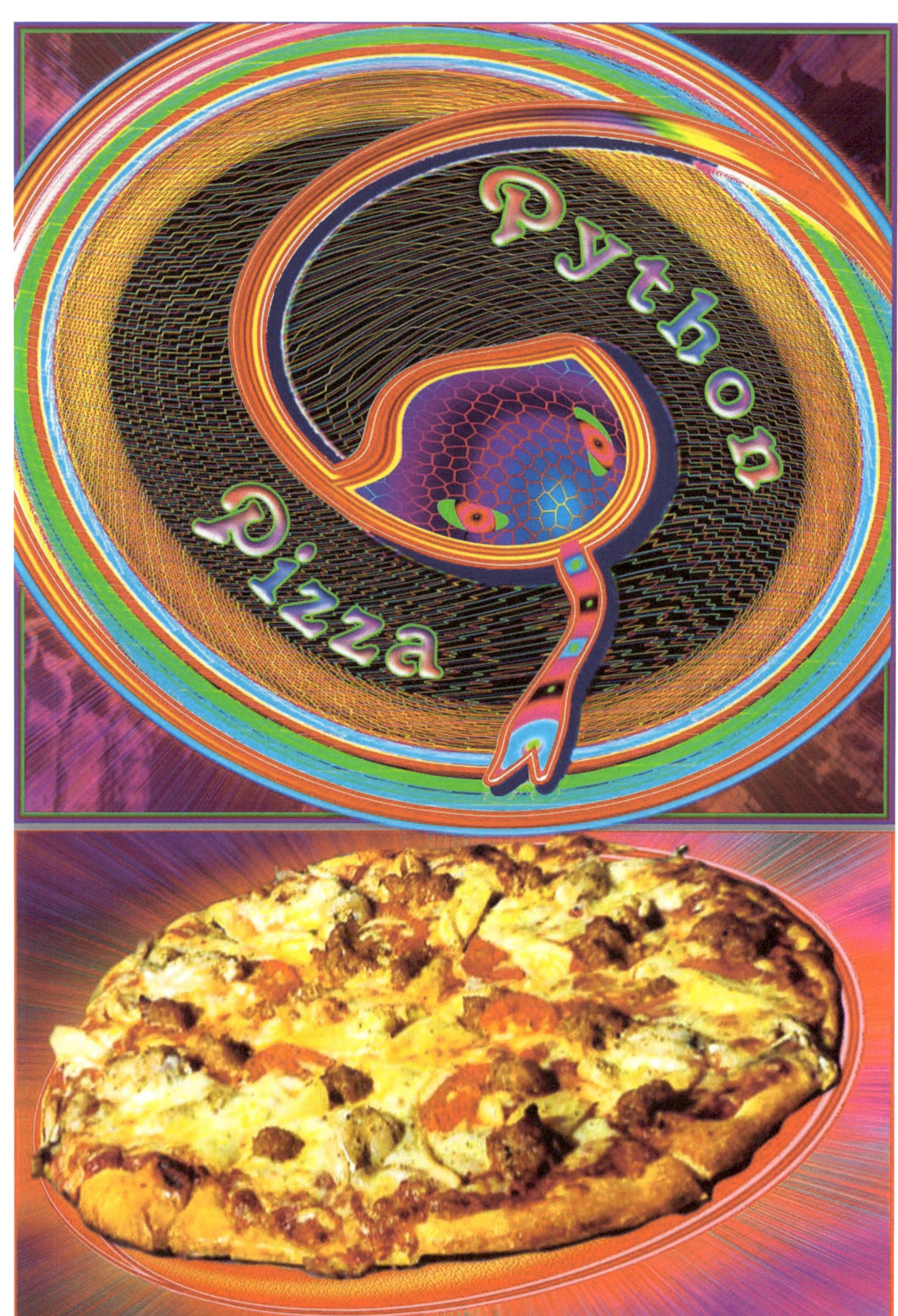

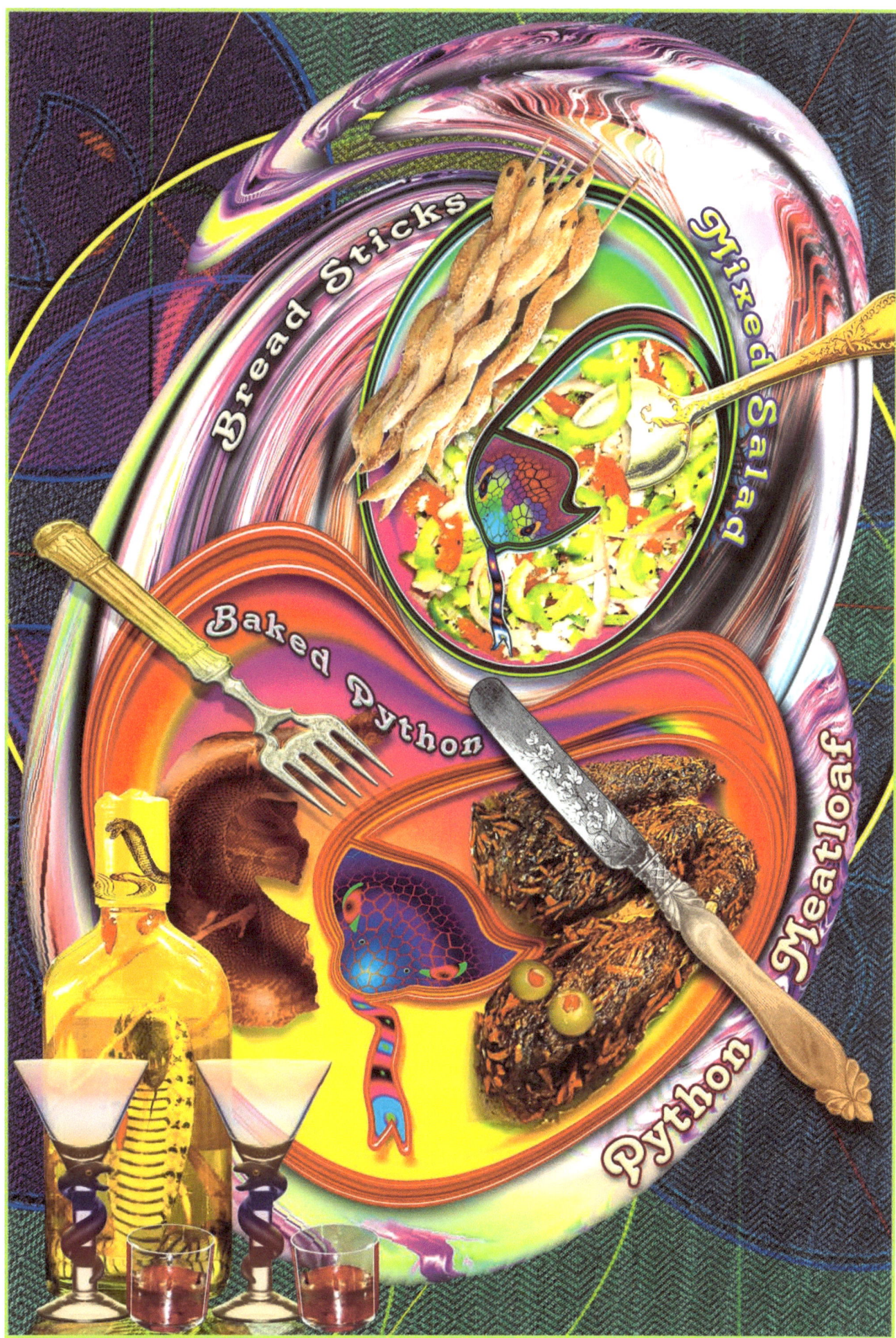

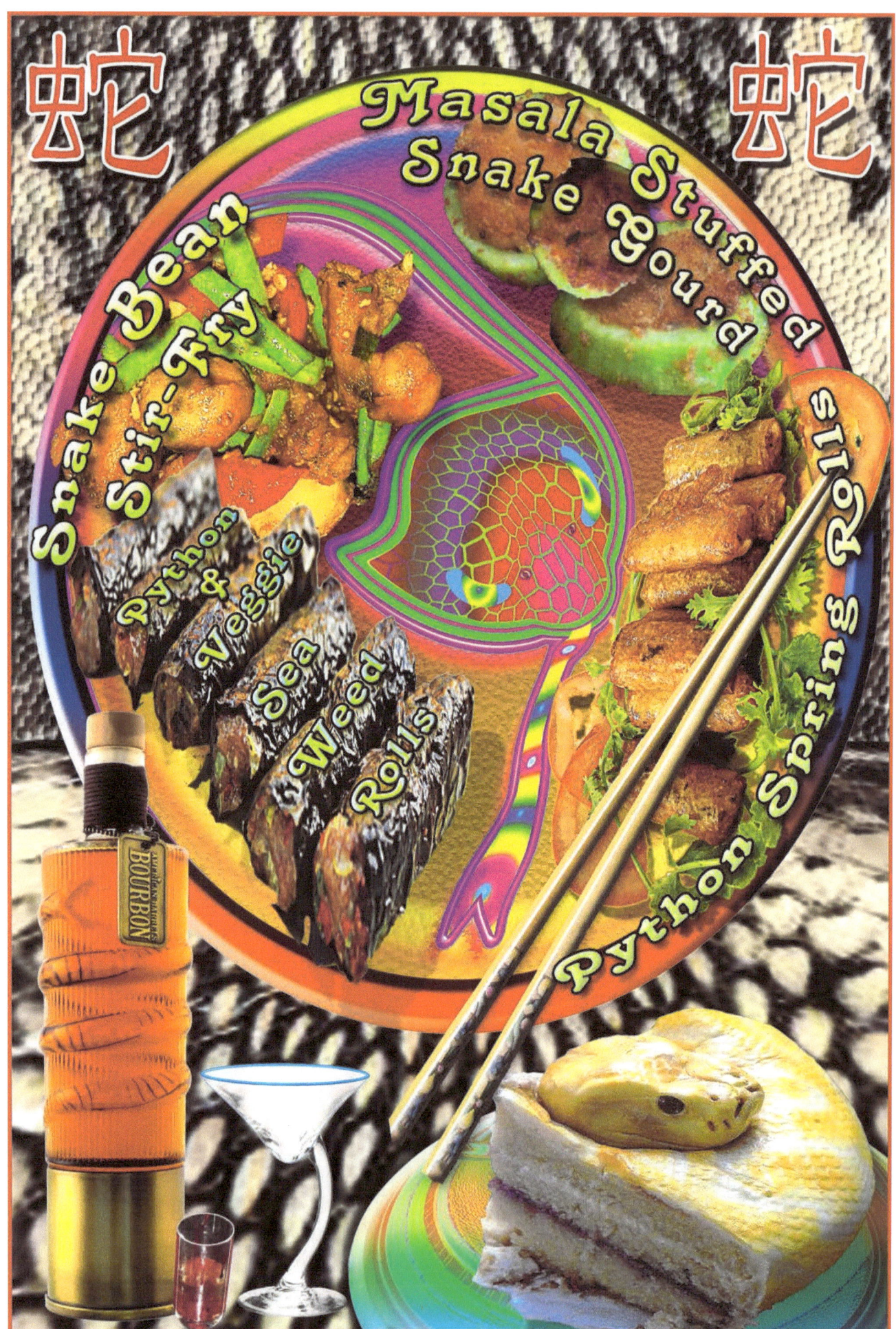

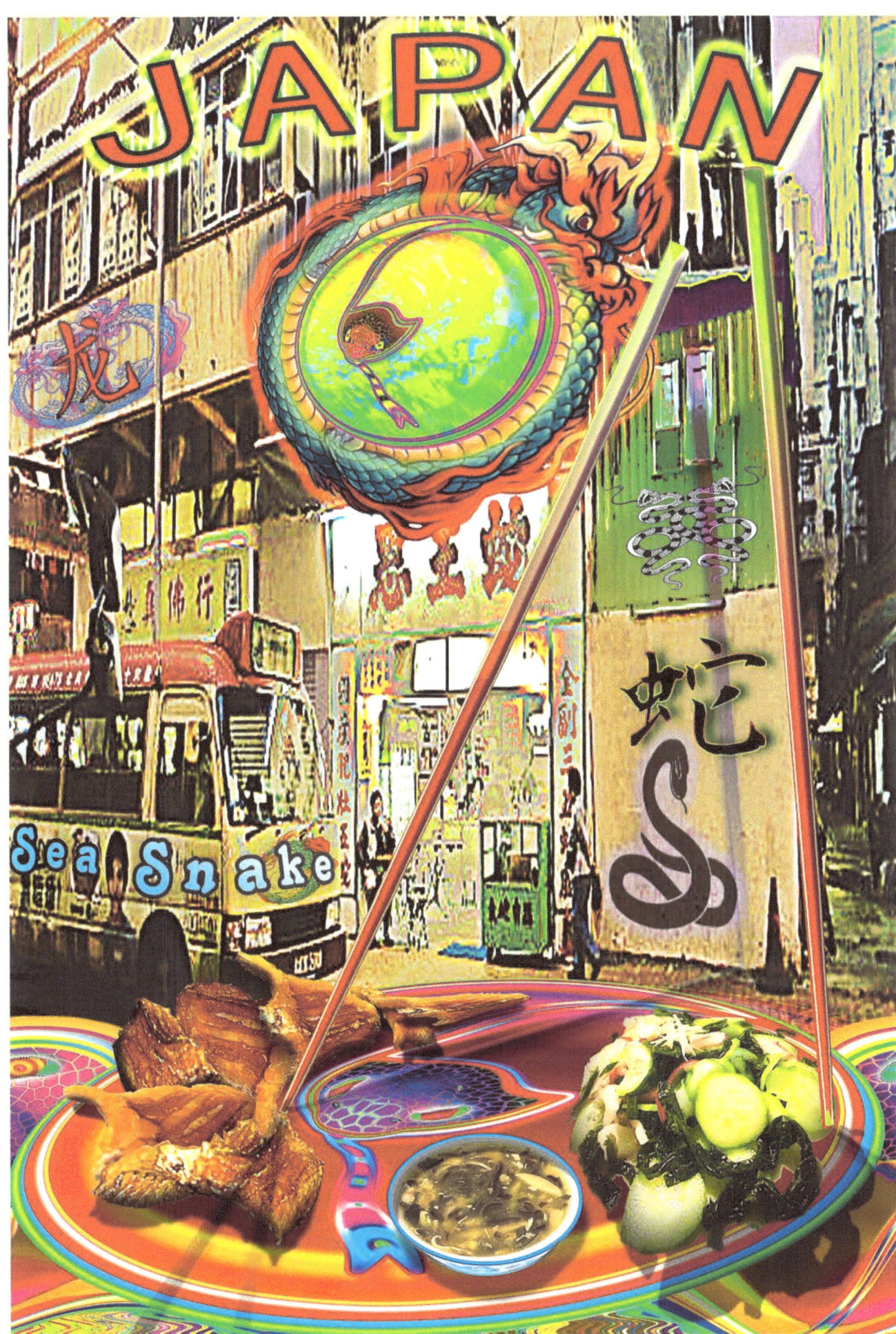

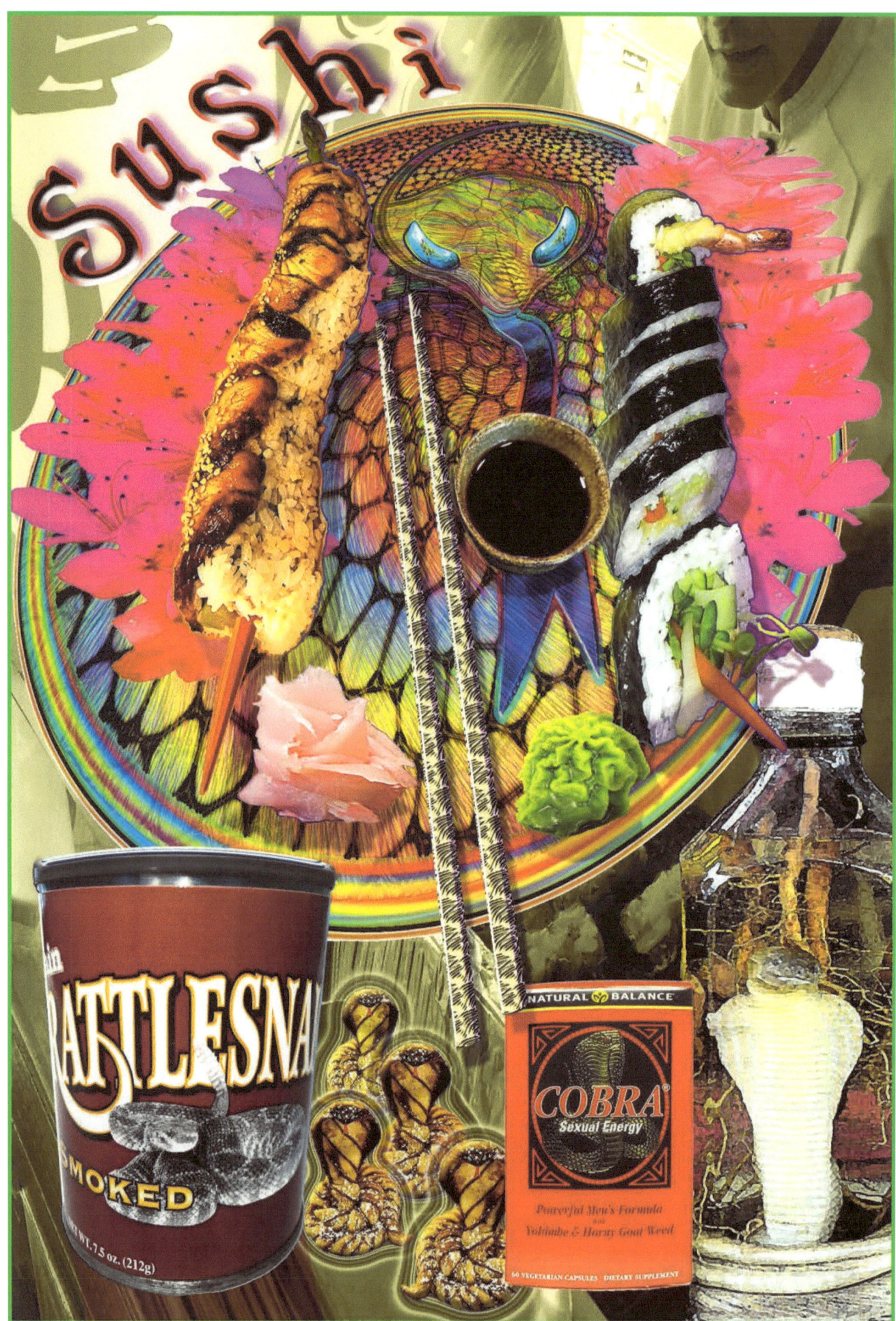

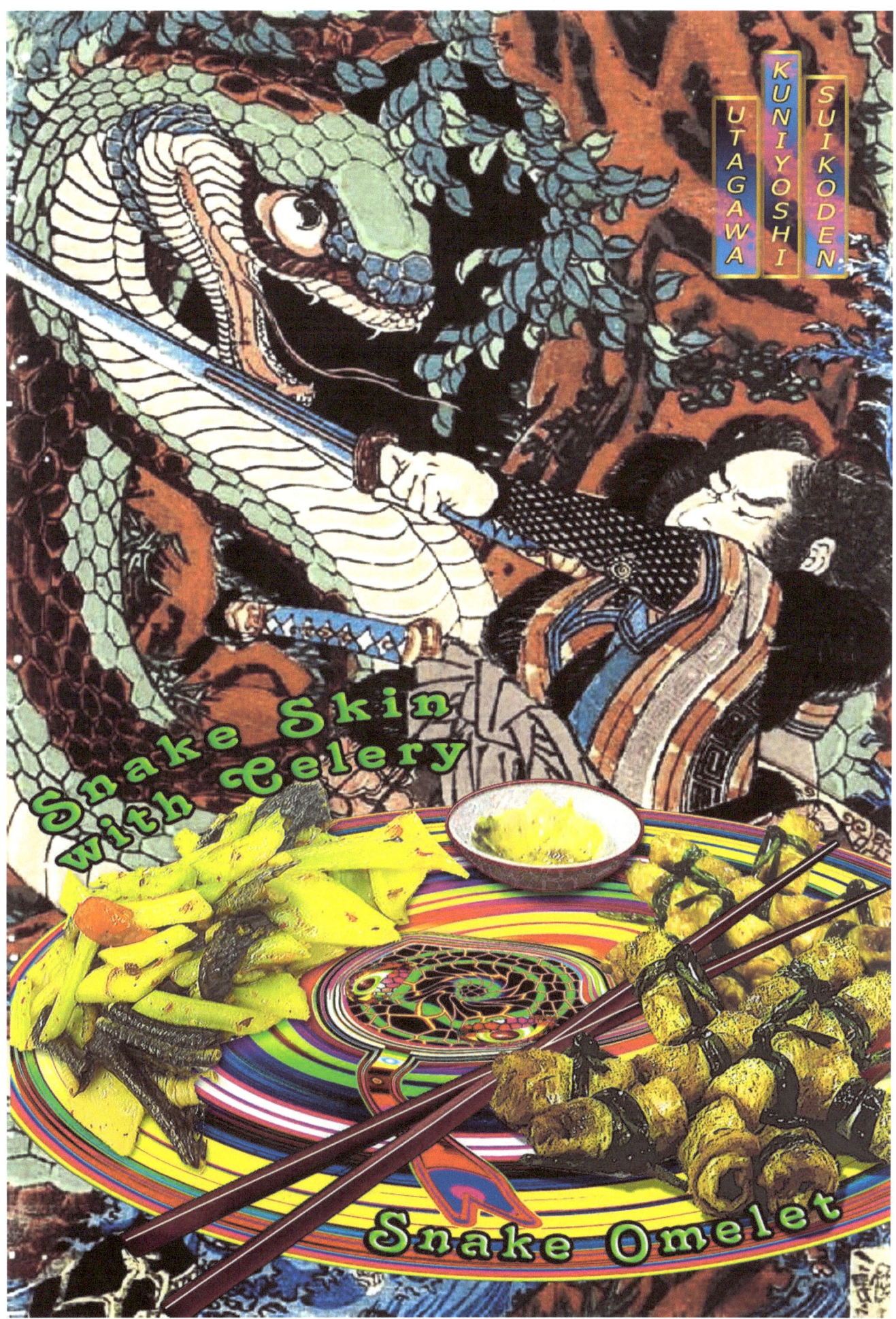

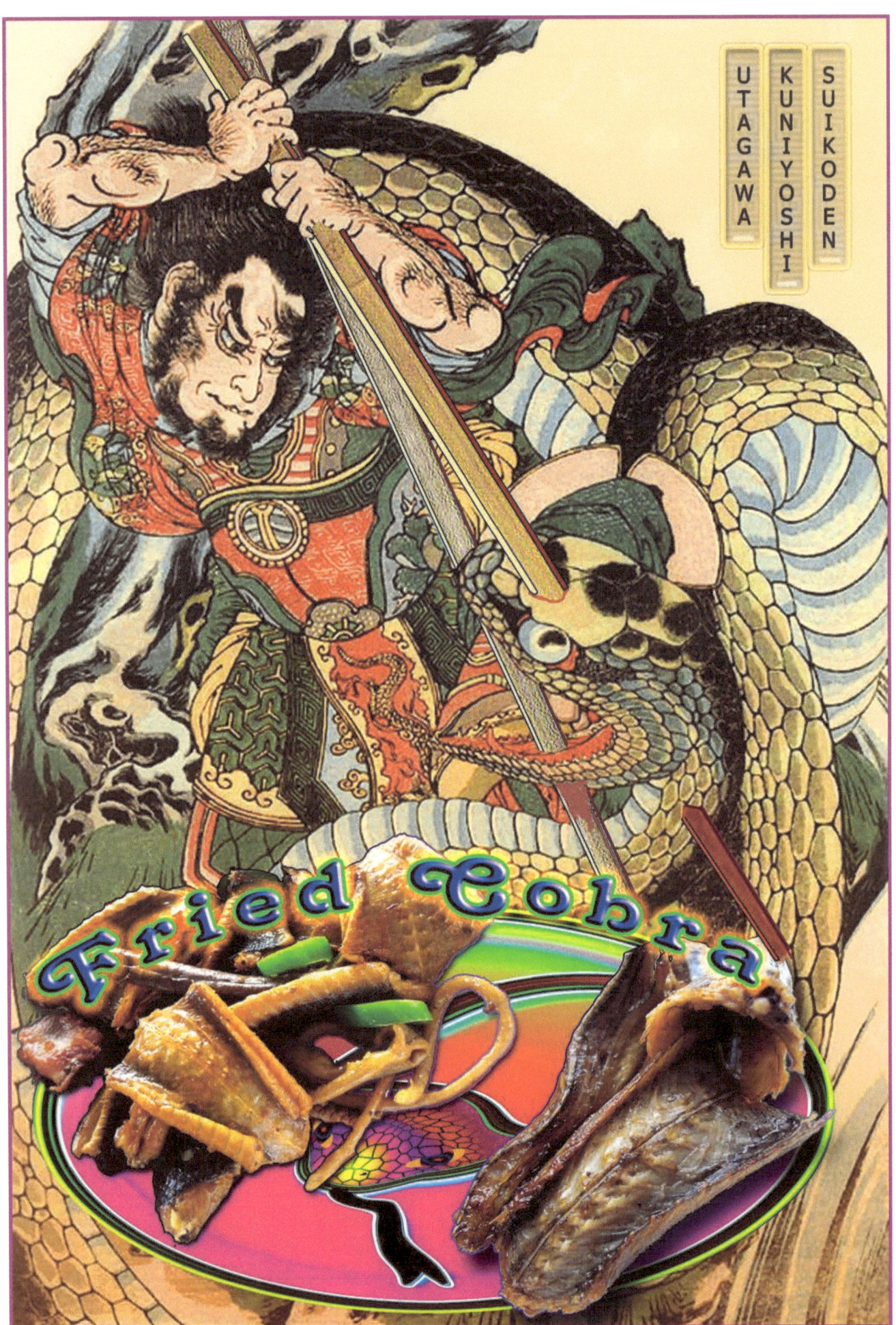

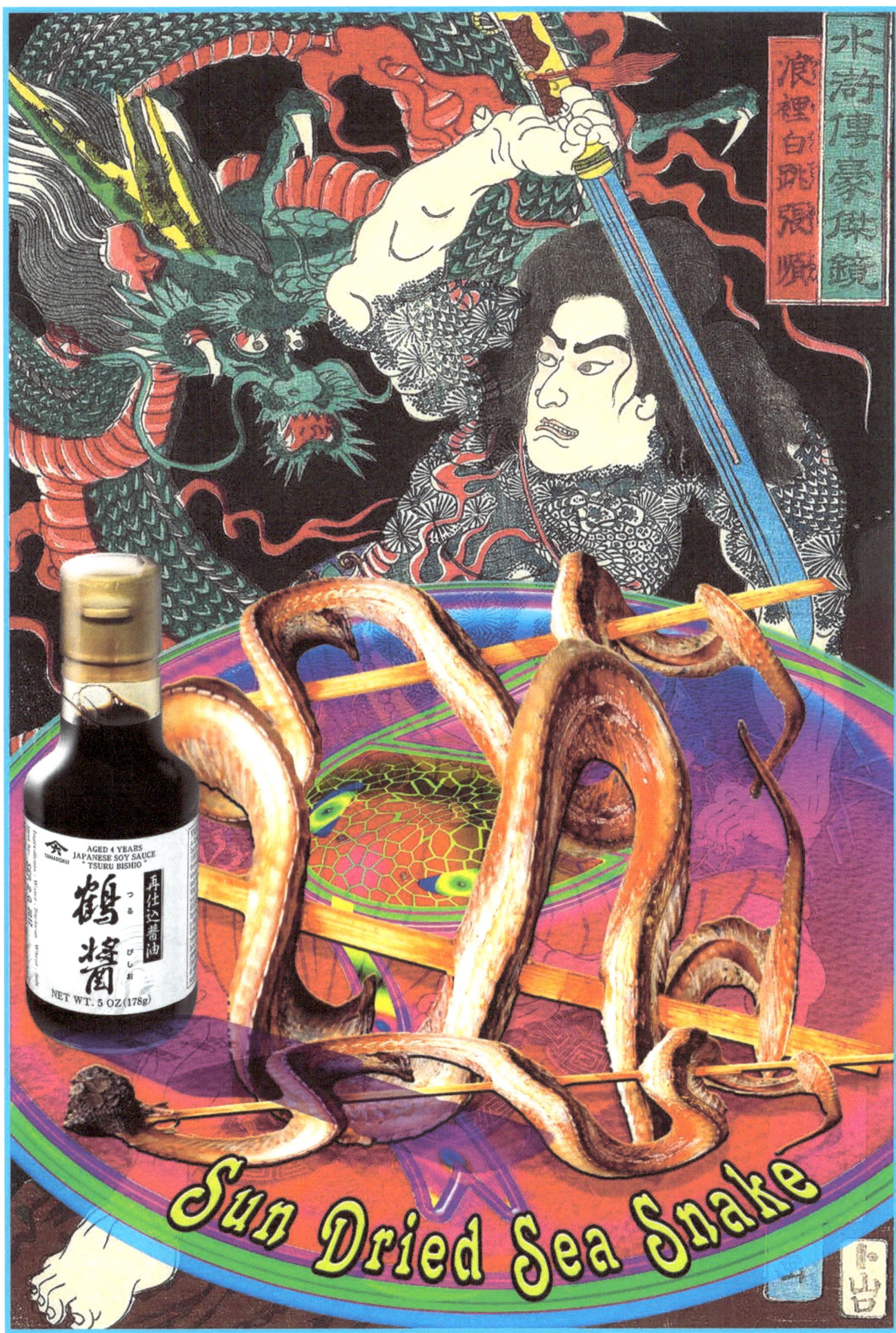

If this book has inspired you to learn more about Snake Cuisine, the ingredients and recipes, and you have a computer that is connected to the internet, then you have an open door to the history and practice of hunting, preparing and consuming snakes. Just GOOGLE "foods that contain Snake Meat" and you'll be on your way to a worldwide, roller-coaster ride through "Snake-land". Following, are just a few web-site locations to get you "slithering" on your journey.

http://www.instructables.com/id/How-to-Skin-and-Clean–a-Dead-Snake/

http://www.millennialhomesteader.com/?p=224

http://www.wikihow.com/Cook-a-Snake/

http://www.http://www.youtube.com/watch?v=FelfDbkzm4

https://en.wikipedia.org/wiki/Black-banded_sea_krait

http://survival-mastery.com/skills/scouting/edible-snakes.html

https://captainhunter.com/how-to-eat-a-snake-safely-and-correctly/

https://walkaboutseasia.wordpress.com/tag/vietnamese-food/

http://bestvietnamtours.info/exotic-food-in-vietnam.php

https://en.wikipedia.org/wiki/Snake_soup

http://www.instructables.com>food>recipes

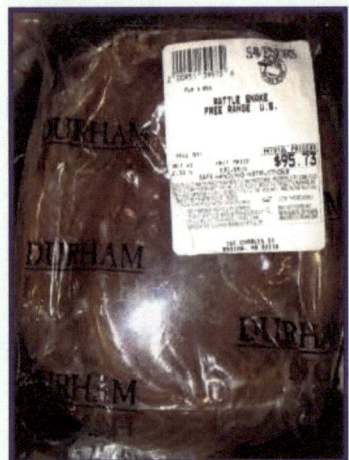

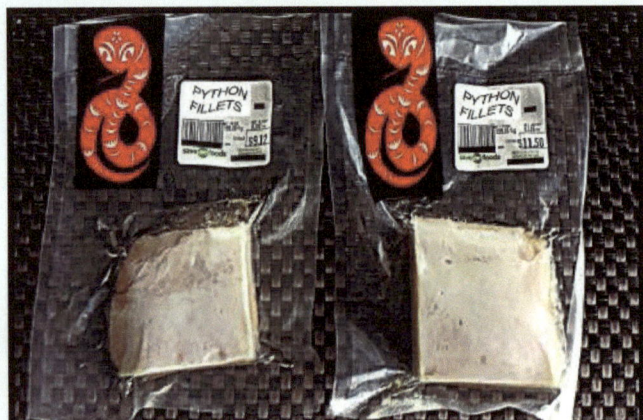

http://www.pinterest.com/explore/rattlesnake-recipe/

https://www.yelp.co.uk/biz

https://www.pbfy.com/fun-information/17-types-of-meat-you-can-use-for-jerky/

http://www.wideopenspaces.com/wild-game-restaurants-across-country-pics/

http://www.dadcooksdinner.com/road-trip-market-district-grand-opening-in-green-oh/

http://www.sierrameat.com

http://www.mountainamericajerky.com

http://www.sales@hillsfoods.com   { Check for availability }

http://www.gmanetwork.com/news/newstv/bestmen/269671/three-snake-recipes-you-have-to-try/story/

Würstküche Restaurant, Los Angeles http://www.wurstruche.com

Tim Love's Lonesome Dove Western Bistro, Fort Worth, TX. http://www.lonesomedovebistro.com KING COBRA Restaurant & Medication: Jalan Mangga Besar Raya No. 93C Tel. +62-21 629-6087

Istana Raja Kobra 24x Valan Ngural Rai bypass, Kuta, Bali, Kuta Indonesia

The Hung Snake Restaurant, Vietnam http://www.thehungsnakeretaurant@gmail.com

Google: Asadachi 1 Chrome-2-14 Nishishinjuku, Shinjuku, Tokyo, Japan

A MESMERIZING PERSONAL ACCOUNT OF USING STREAM OF CONSCIOUSNESS ART-MAKING TO RE-DISCOVER DETAILS OF A HALF-FORGOTTEN VISAGE FROM AN INTRIGUING DREAM.

NOW AVAILABLE ON LINE

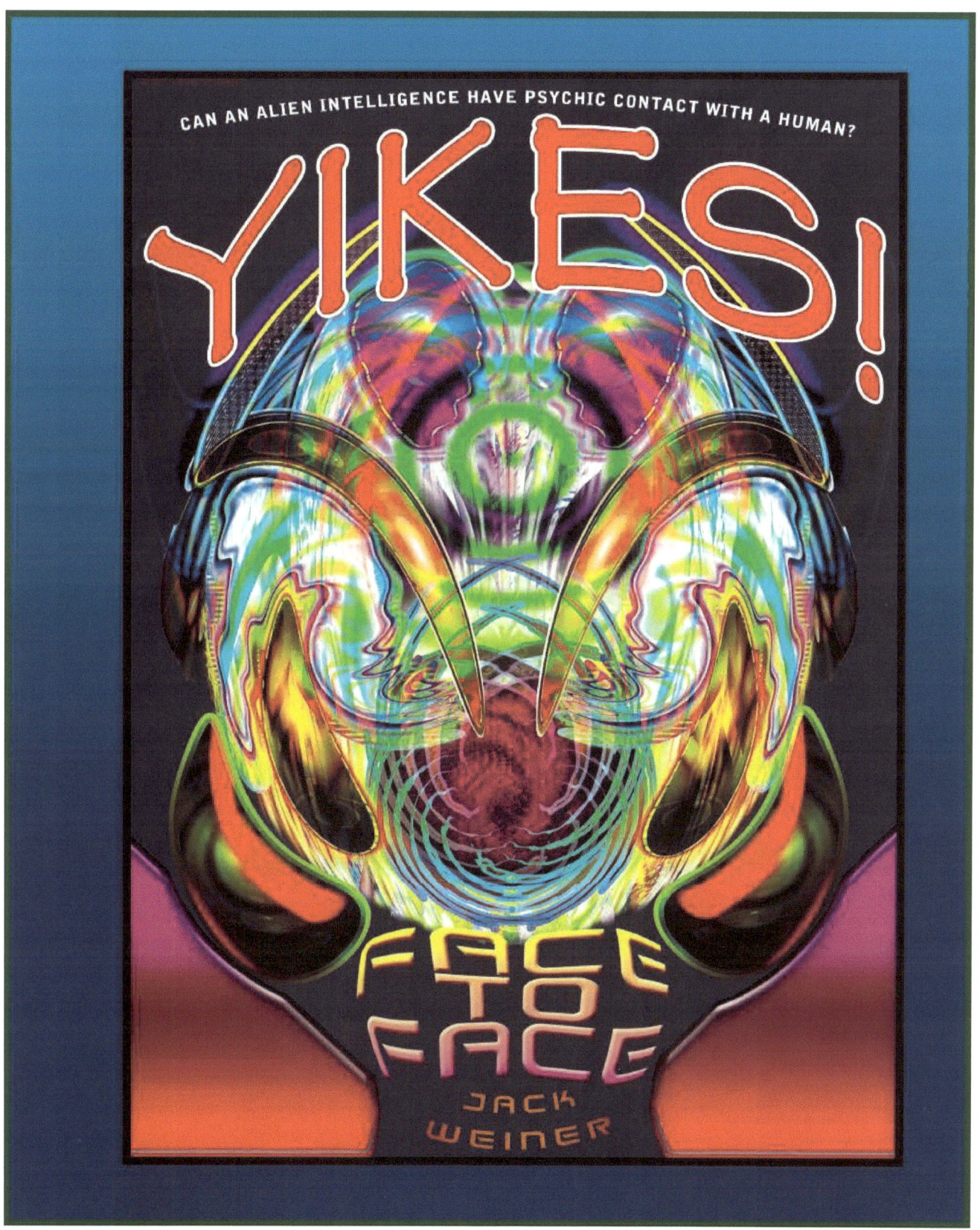

You may wonder why anyone in their right mind would make a book such as this. The answer to that is not difficult to fathom...I **am** out of my mind; well, almost. At the least, spending more than a year and several thousand hours doing research and designing this book on my computer, has caused me to become noticeably more **"SSSSSnaaaakiiiiieeeerrrr".** Just part of the territory; it will wear off soon...I guesssssssssss!

Truth be told, I have eaten Rattlesnake. When I was a child, my father and uncles would go up to Pennsylvania's Pocono Mts. and gather wild Huckleberries. The vast patches of ripe berries would attract a wide variety of insects, small birds and rodents; preferred prey for several species of snakes, including Rattlesnakes. So, by the time a large wash-tub was filled with berries, they would also have "bagged" one or two good sized "Rattlers" to bring back for my Aunts frying pan. It was considered a delicacy when dipped in a "beer batter", fried and served with corn on the cob, fried potatoes and crispy onion rings.

So, are all snakes edible for people? What about the very poisonous one's? Who in their right mind would eat snakes? Those are all valid questions. In fact those are the very same subjects that I addressed when I decided to start the research for this book. I must confess, that once I went on-line and began searching "Snake Cuisine", I was amazed by the abundant informational web sites about various species of snakes; as well as, many links to foreign and domestic gastronomical recipes that I was able to uncover. As it turned out, the shear number of snake cuisine dishes, soups, and stews was a good thing, for it gave me plenty of ideas as to what I could put on my "Snakes on Plates" ceramic plate designs that I had spent over a year creating on my personal computer. It seemed like the perfect combination; "Snake Cuisine" on a "Snake Plate".

My undying gratitude to:

My most patient wife, Mary.

My brother Jim for his editing prowess.

My friend Rick for his encouragement.

www.ingramcontent.com/pod-product-compliance
Lightning Source LLC
Chambersburg PA
CBHW040416220526
45473CB00004B/1263